MEN'S BODY SCULPTING

Nick Evans, MD

HUMAN KINETICS

Library of Congress Cataloging-in-Publication Data

Evans, Nick, 1964-
    Men's body sculpting / Nick Evans.
        p. cm.
Includes bibliographical references (p.) and index.
    ISBN 0-7360-5141-4
    1. Bodybuilding.   I. Title.
    GV546.5.E83   2004
    613.7'13--dc22

                                        2003019627

ISBN-10: 0-7360-5141-4
ISBN-13: 978-0-7360-5141-5

Acquisitions Editor: Martin Barnard; **Developmental Editor:** Cynthia McEntire; **Assistant Editor:** Scott Hawkins; **Copyeditor:** John Wentworth; **Proofreader:** Julie Marx Goodreau; **Indexer:** Susan Danzi Hernandez; **Graphic Designer:** Robert Reuther; **Graphic Artist:** Sandra Meier; **Photo Manager:** Dan Wendt; **Cover Designer:** Jack W. Davis; **Photographer (cover):** Davy Kirkpatrick; **Photographers (interior):** Ralph DeHaan, Davy Kirkpatrick; **Printer:** United Graphics

We thank the Los Angeles Trade Technical College and World Gym in Lake Forest, California, for assistance in providing the locations for the photo shoots for this book.

Human Kinetics books are available at special discounts for bulk purchase. Special editions or book excerpts can also be created to specification. For details, contact the Special Sales Manager at Human Kinetics.

Printed in the United States of America

10   9   8   7

Human Kinetics
Web site: www.HumanKinetics.com

United States: Human Kinetics
P.O. Box 5076
Champaign, IL 61825-5076
800-747-4457
e-mail: humank@hkusa.com

Canada: Human Kinetics
475 Devonshire Road Unit 100
Windsor, ON N8Y 2L5
800-465-7301 (in Canada only)
e-mail: orders@hkcanada.com

Europe: Human Kinetics
107 Bradford Road
Stanningley
Leeds LS28 6AT, United Kingdom
+44 (0) 113 255 5665
e-mail: hk@hkeurope.com

Australia: Human Kinetics
57A Price Avenue
Lower Mitcham, South Australia 5062
08 8277 1555
e-mail: liaw@hkaustralia.com

New Zealand: Human Kinetics
Division of Sports Distributors NZ Ltd.
P.O. Box 300 226 Albany
North Shore City
Auckland
0064 9 448 1207
e-mail: info@humankinetics.co.nz

contents

preface

Picture the perfect body, the kind of body you really want. Now hold that thought. What do you see? A sleek six-pack? Awesome arms? Bold shoulders and a chiseled chest? An image of physical perfection? Well, that dream body *could* be yours. The secret is right here in this book.

All you must do is make a simple decision, right here, right now. You have two choices: one, put the book down and walk away empty-handed, or two, take the book home and absorb the power within its pages.

It's a no-brainer, really, but think for a minute anyway. It's no coincidence that this book caught your eye, that you picked it from the shelf, that you're holding it in your hands, and that I have your attention. It's your destiny. It's your right to have the body you want, and now you have the opportunity, the chance to change, to turn your dream body into reality, to become a sculpture of living flesh and blood with bulging muscles shredding your clothes from the inside.

You'd like that, wouldn't you? Imagine a tight torso bringing a smile to your face every time you look in the mirror. Think about turning heads as you walk down the street. Think of it. What have you got to lose? Nothing ventured, nothing gained, right? Unlock the door to your true potential. Make a difference before it's too late.

Okay, time's up. You decide. What's it going to be? Read the book and say hello to your new custom-built body or . . . well, there isn't really another option, is there? You know it's time to get the body you want. It's a decision you'll never regret. Within these pages you'll find everything you want to know about building a stronger, leaner, more muscular physique.

As of yet, there's no magic pill for developing a body of armor. (If you know of one, can you pick me up a lifetime supply?) You can't gulp down the latest nutritional supplement and expect an instant transformation. You can't just walk into a department store on Memorial Day and buy a fashionable physique for the summer. There's more to gaining muscle than walking through the doors of a gym, listening to the clang of iron, the whir of stationary bikes, and the grunts of other people bench pressing.

Would you like the help of a special instructor? If so, which of the following teachers would you choose: a personal trainer with over 20 years of in-the-gym experience, a personal physician with an intimate knowledge of bodybuilding who practices what he preaches and leads by example, a personal fitness guru who has a monthly advice column in a top-selling bodybuilding magazine, or a personal nutritionist who is a spokesman for a major sport nutrition company? Tough choice. Well, that's okay because you don't have to make the choice. You can have them all.

I know that you know your way around a gym. But if you're tired of spending countless hours pumping iron with little or no change in your physique, this book will save you time, effort, and money by revealing the most direct route to your physical perfection. End your frustration and start achieving results in a fraction of the time. Make no mistake—this isn't a pop-up picture book of exercises or a quick-fix boot camp for couch potatoes. This is the real deal; basic training is over and we're on the battlefield. So, lock and load your muscles. Take aim at your body fat and get ready for a massive attack. Your mission—if you choose to accept it—is staged in three integrated steps.

In part I, you'll be equipped with the complete package to maximize muscle mass. Right away you'll learn the best exercise techniques to scientifically stimulate muscle growth. The next time you set foot in the gym, you'll have a *new* set of rules to lift by, with brutal assault tactics to raise the intensity level of your workouts. Armed with these trade secrets, you'll have no excuse for not reaching your potential. The focused contraction technique (chapter 2)—unique to this book—is the ultimate muscle-building stimulus. Every rep and every set of every workout serve a specific purpose. Muscle growth requires an anabolic environment, a state that promotes tissue repair. In chapter 3, you'll learn 12 simple steps toward gaining an anabolic advantage and optimizing your body's testosterone level. More testosterone means more muscle and a supercharged sex drive. The mass generator program (chapter 4) is my personal prescription for packing on pounds of muscle fast. Each exercise is hand picked to induce a surge in size.

In part II, you'll learn the best methods for cutting body fat. Building muscles is one thing; seeing them is another. Get the skinny on body fat in chapter 5, and learn the best weapons to torch your fat stores with extreme prejudice. That lean, mean, muscle machine will be yours, maybe sooner than you think. In these pages, you'll find a complete nutrition package for the hard body. Exercise requires high-grade muscle fuel. For the bodybuilder, the challenge is to provide the right nutrients to feed muscle growth while starving the fat stores at the same time. Let me show you winning recipes for a hard muscle diet and my secret ingredients for getting that shredded six-pack (chapter 6). The body fat blitz program (chapter 7) is tailored to melt away fat and get you that lean body look.

Part III gives you the advanced tools you need for chiseling the ultimate body. I'll teach you how to integrate your workouts and your diet for maximum benefit—the secret combination that makes the magic. Climb the 12 steps up the ladder of intensity in chapter 8 to discover how to turn up the heat at the gym.

Train beyond pain and enter the zone of hyperintensity, pushing your muscles past the point of failure to generate extreme muscular development. What about anabolic steroids? Look no further. The real deal is revealed in chapter 9—the good, the bad, and the ugly truth about these muscle-building drugs. Are there safer ways to fuel your intensified workouts? You bet. I've put together a super supplement stack for sure-fire results (chapter 10). Find out which nutritional aids work and how to use them effectively. The hybrid hard body program (chapter 11) is my personal formula for the ultimate physique. This program is an advanced system designed to build, shape, and sculpt your torso by maximizing muscle growth and fat loss at the same time. Finally, in chapter 12, I present survival strategies for the peak physique, skills that make muscle maintenance easy. You'll learn how to prevent pitfalls in your progress, fix faults in your physique, and burst out of any training plateau. This chapter also gives you a doctor's own recipe for muscle care and tips for treating and preventing injury.

If you're one of the millions of people worldwide who work out, this is a book you can't afford to be without. It's a must for your gym bag. Everything you need to know to tweak your technique and fine tune your physique is in these pages. Life is not a dress rehearsal. There's no rewind button. You get only one body, one chance, and the clock is ticking. What are you waiting for?

acknowledgments

I wish to thank the following individuals for their help on this book:

- ▶ Human Kinetics for making this project an absolute joy from start to finish, especially Martin Barnard for his creative guidance and Cynthia McEntire for fine-tuning the text.
- ▶ Ralph DeHaan and Davy Kirkpatrick for their enthusiastic photography; Julien, Chris, and Adam for helping demonstrate the exercises; and Los Angeles Trade Technical College and World Gym (Lake Forest, California) for providing the photo shoot locations.
- ▶ Robert Kennedy for inviting me to write *MuscleMag*'s "Ask the Doctor" column; *MuscleTech* for providing nutritional supplements that work; and Gold's Gym (Venice, California) for inspiring my workouts.
- ▶ William Stanish, MD, Douglas Jackson, MD, and James Luck, MD, for mentoring my career in orthopedic surgery.
- ▶ My family—Valerie, Gwyn, Luc, Daniel, and Sera—for their lifelong support; Michael and Jennifer for introducing me to America; and MG for over a decade of loving encouragement and inspiration.

PART I

MAXIMIZING MUSCLE MASS

chapter 1

MASS CONSTRUCTION

It seems like a simple concept—lift weights to make your muscles grow bigger and stronger—but there's so much more to it than meets the eye. In fact, one could say, "You think you know about muscle growth? You have no idea!"

For instance, when it comes to maximizing muscle growth, do you know how many repetitions you should perform or how much weight you should lift? Should you lift the weight slowly or quickly? What is the optimal number of sets? How long should you rest between sets? How long does it take for your muscles to recover between workouts? What's happening inside your muscles when they grow? What exactly does "intensity" mean? What is momentary muscular failure?

You might know your way around a weight room, and you've probably spent countless hours working out, but have you ever stopped to think about precisely what you're doing and why you're doing it that way? It's easy to switch on auto-pilot and cruise through your workout, but is your routine really working for you? Are you seeing changes in your physique? Or, are you frustrated with your lack of progress?

Instead of going nowhere with the same old business-as-usual training routine, maybe it's time to pause and gather your thoughts. Take a class on muscle mass. After all, if you know why muscles grow, you'll understand how to make it happen. Remember that your body is a masterpiece of biology—learn to work with nature, not against it.

I'll show you what works and what doesn't so that you won't get stuck in first gear at the gym. Using my five-point checklist, you'll be able to systematically evaluate your workouts and tune up your training technique like a master mechanic. The next time you hit the gym, you'll drive through the doors with a new set of rules to lift by and sure-fire tactics for monster mass.

WHAT MONEY CAN'T BUY

Recall the credit card commercial on TV that lists a bunch of purchases and their values? In your case, the ad would probably go something like this:

Gym membership—$395; lifting belt—$39; tight tank top—$25; latest nutritional supplement—$46; shredding your shirt sleeve with bulging biceps—priceless!

MUSCLE GROWTH

Muscle growth requires three things: stimulus, fuel, and repair. The stimulus—exercise—makes the muscle work, drains its energy store, and causes microscopic damage to the muscle fibers. After exercise, the muscle must replenish its fuel tank and repair itself. Provided that the stimulus was of sufficient intensity, the muscle will adapt (grow) during the repair process.

Muscle adapts to exercise so that it is better equipped and functionally more effective when it receives the next bout of exercise. The three types of adaptation are neural, hypertrophic, and metabolic. An increase in muscle strength is largely due to neural adaptation, which enhances the muscle's electrical supply. The nerve impulses fire more quickly and recruit more muscle fibers, resulting in a more powerful muscular contraction. Initial strength gains from weight training reflect neural adaptations; but, in the long term, improvements in strength are secondary to an increase in muscle size. In other words, strength follows size.

An increase in muscle size is due to hypertrophic adaptation, which results in an increase in the cross-sectional area of individual muscle fibers. Exercise-induced hypertrophy affects fast-twitch type II (strength) fibers more than it affects slow-twitch type I (endurance) fibers. So as the muscle gets bigger, it becomes stronger.

During metabolic adaptation, the muscle's biochemical profile evolves to improve oxygen and energy use. This process improves muscular endurance.

The strength–endurance continuum is a theory that explains how muscle undergoes a specific adaptation to an imposed demand. At one end, strength training induces primarily neural adaptations; at the opposite end, endurance training causes metabolic changes. Hypertrophic adaptations are induced by training methods that exist somewhere between the two extremes—hence, the concept of task specificity. If you want pure muscle strength, train like a weightlifter. If you prefer muscular endurance, train like a long-distance runner. If your primary goal is size, your muscle requires a different set of imposed demands. You don't want your muscle to adapt via purely neural pathways or metabolic pathways. What you need is hypertrophic adaptation, which creates bigger muscles, more mass, and monster size.

To generate a hypertrophic response, the exercise stimulus must be intense. Exercise intensity is the degree of effort or percent of momentary ability. At the point of momentary muscular failure, 100 percent effort intensity is required to complete the last rep. The muscle is pushed to its functional limit

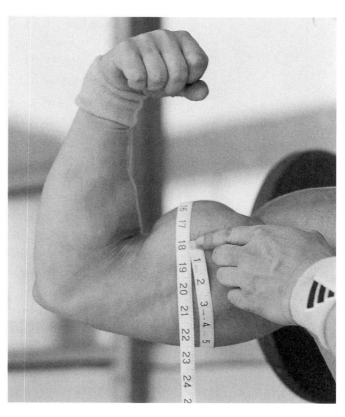

Hypertrophic adaptation explains why muscles get larger with exercise.

and must contract to its maximum capability to complete the task. Performing a set to failure generates 100 percent intensity, and the magnitude of this huge stimulus results in hypertrophic adaptation. If you want muscular growth, you must work the muscle to the point of failure.

During exercise, muscle gets its energy from a substance called adenosine triphosphate (ATP). This unit of energy has three sources—phosphocreatine, glycogen, and oxygen—that act in sequence, like a trail of dominos. When you begin your first repetition, phosphocreatine provides the energy. This stuff is stored inside muscle, ready for action, but its supply lasts only up to 10 seconds. After that point, glycogen takes over as the energy provider. The chemical conversion of glycogen releases lactic acid as a by-product, and it's this build-up of acid in the muscle that inflicts a burning pain and leads to fatigue within two to three minutes.

These first two energy sources are anaerobic—that is, they do not require oxygen. At the completion of one set to failure, your fatigued muscles scream with the pain of excess acid. Your breathing gets heavy as you gasp for the third source of energy—oxygen. Blood flow into the muscle increases, delivering the much-needed oxygen to relieve the oxygen debt and wash out the lactic acid build-up. This rush of blood inflates the muscle like a balloon, causing the phenomenon known as the muscle pump.

An intense set of repetitions performed to the point of muscular failure is an insult to the muscle. Not only does it deplete the muscle's energy store, but it also causes microscopic damage to the muscle tissue. These disrupted muscle fibers cause delayed-onset muscle soreness, the muscular pain that peaks a day or two after intense exercise. During the recovery phase, the muscle's energy stores of glycogen and phosphocreatine are restocked from dietary carbohydrates and creatine. The damaged muscle fibers are repaired by protein synthesis using dietary amino acids. The repair process regenerates a bigger muscle fiber.

Fiber disruption is essential for muscular hypertrophy. It takes five to seven days to repair the muscle damage induced by high-intensity weight training. After an all-out assault on your muscles, an adequate period of rest is essential if you want to build those muscle fibers!

The general adaptation syndrome theory suggests that a body system will adapt with improved function when faced with a stress to which it is not accustomed. This concept implies that when the neuromuscular system is overloaded, it adapts to match the stress, but if the stress is left unchanged over time, adaptation will reach a plateau. The principle of overload is of paramount importance if you want to continue growing muscle. That's why lifting weights is properly termed progressive resistance training. Once your muscle adapts to lifting a certain weight, you make it work harder by progressing to the next level of stimulus by increasing the resistance. If you do not elicit an overload effect, hypertrophic adaptation will cease. Adaptation to a training stimulus deteriorates within two weeks of exposure. To maximize neuromuscular adaptation, the stimulus—such as load—should be increased every two to three weeks.

Now that you know why muscles grow, your next step is to put the principles you have learned into practice. At this point, we'll discuss what you have to do at the gym to generate the precise stimulus that induces hypertrophic adaptation in your muscle.

RULES TO LIFT BY

For even the simplest task there are usually several ways to get the job done. Let's say I give you three objects: a hammer, a nail, and a piece of wood. How will you go about hitting the nail into the wood? Maybe you'll take the cautious approach and hit the nail repetitively with many gentle taps of the hammer, sinking the nail into the wood slowly but surely, taking five minutes to complete the task. Alternatively, you could strike the nail a single time with all your might, sinking it into the wood with one huge blow, completing the task in one second. The second approach is far quicker in terms of time and effort, but there's an element of risk involved. If you miss the nail, you might bring the hammer crashing down onto your thumb with a painful thump. And that would be the end of hammering for a while.

Like driving a nail into wood, training with weights has several possible techniques. Too little weight, and the exercise is ineffective—you'd get more of a workout washing your car. Too much weight, and you could wind up in the emergency room with a torn muscle. What we need is middle ground. Let's sift through the bodybuilder's tool box and select the best tools to construct your body effectively and safely.

Before you start work on your body, we'll first analyze the principles of weight training. Why? Because manipulating the basic principles is the key to fine-tuning your physique. Minor details make all the difference, and the secrets lie within the fine print. Tweaking your technique involves making adjustments to every aspect of your exercise program, including your number of repetitions, amount of weight, number of sets, combination of exercises, rest intervals, and workout time.

If you want to make progress, pay close attention to detail. Imagine building your dream house. You start with simple raw materials and, brick by brick, construct your perfect palace with a solid foundation from the ground up. This is how we'll create the framework of your exercise program. Each stage is critical within the architecture of the final construct; I'll explain why as we go along.

To create a mass-building regime that works, follow these five points: precision repetition, work set, rest interval, workout time, and recovery. Each point serves to focus your attention on the essential details required to stimulate the maximum hypertrophic adaptation from your muscles.

Precision Repetition

The repetition, or rep, is the basic building block of any workout. Two aspects of the repetition need careful consideration: quality and quantity.

The quality of a repetition is determined by its execution, or the time taken to lift and lower the weight. The speed at which the rep is performed is called the repetition cadence or tempo.

Each repetition has three phases: lower, pause, and lift. The gold standard repetition cadence uses a two-second lowering phase, a one-second pause, and a two-second lift phase. This 2-1-2 repetition cadence requires five seconds to complete the full range of motion. A very quick repetition cadence, such as a 1-1 (no pause phase), typically allows the use of a heavier weight because of the rapid acceleration during the movement. However, quick-cadence reps actually decrease intensity because excessive momentum is introduced. A rapid movement may allow for the demonstration of strength by literally throwing the weight, but this is not the optimal way to build muscle mass.

Stimulating muscle growth requires repetitions performed in a slow, precise cadence. The movement you want can be compared to the action of a spring. On the way down, the spring is being compressed. Upon reaching the bottom, the spring releases its force in a smooth upward motion. The precision repetition is controlled and smooth, never bounced, jerked, or done with momentum. This ensures that the muscle is in a state of contraction at all times. In other words, the muscle must be kept under tension throughout the movement. It's the time under tension that provides the stimulus for muscle growth. During each rep, be sure to focus your mind on the muscle contracting and nothing else.

The phases of the precision rep evolve from scientific principles. There are three types of muscle contraction: concentric, isometric, and eccentric. To gain the maximum benefit from each repetition, your muscle should experience all three types of contraction. As an example, consider this simple task. When you raise a cup from a table to your mouth, your biceps is performing a concentric, or positive, contraction. When you lower the cup back to the table, your biceps is performing an eccentric, or negative, contraction. If you hold the cup still as you walk across the kitchen, your biceps is performing an isometric, or static, contraction. Why are these distinctions important? Because your biceps muscle must work during all three phases or else you will drop the cup.

The positive (concentric) contraction is actually the weakest of the three types. Your muscle can lower more weight than it can hold still. Your muscle can hold more weight than it can lift. Thus, an eccentric contraction is stronger than an isometric contraction, which in turn is stronger than a concentric contraction. Note what happens as you perform a biceps curl. When your biceps fails during the concentric phase and you can't lift the weight any further, you can still hold the weight at that point. Then, when the isometric contraction fatigues and you can't hold the weight any longer, you are still able to lower the weight under control because the eccentric contraction is stronger.

This is the science behind a precision rep. Performing the repetition in a slow, controlled manner means you do not waste muscular contraction. You make the best use of the negative, static, and positive portions of the rep. Furthermore, slowing down repetition cadence is a method of increasing intensity.

Along with the quality of the repetition, you consider the quantity of the repetition, which involves two factors: how many reps to perform and how much weight to use.

Within the muscle, muscle fibers contract under the all-or-nothing principle. In other words, fibers either contract or they don't. Contraction is not a matter of degree. It's like striking a match—either the flame ignites or it doesn't. To move any given object, your muscle contracts just enough of its fibers to get the job done. For example, your biceps must only contract a few fibers to raise an 8-ounce beverage, but it must bring more fibers into action to lift a 30-pound (13.6-kg) weight. To lift the heaviest possible weight, your muscle must contract all of its fibers. When this happens, the muscle receives its maximum stimulus. Maximum stimulus leads to maximum adaptation.

As discussed previously, a muscle's response to stimulation involves neural (strength), hypertrophic (size), and metabolic (endurance) adaptation. Repetitions must be performed to the point of muscular failure to elicit the maximum response. As the number of repetitions increases, the adaptive response shifts from strength to hypertrophy and then to endurance. Performing a single-repetition maximum (1RM) induces a neural adaptation that increases muscle strength. A six- to eight-repetition maximum causes a hypertrophic response that develops muscle size. When the number of repetitions climbs into double figures, the muscle experiences more of an endurance stimulus, which fails to evoke significant adaptations in size or strength.

Scientific studies indicate that the optimal hypertrophy training protocol uses a set of six to eight repetitions performed to the point of muscular failure using the heaviest possible load. The best stimulus for inducing maximum muscular hypertrophy is to lift a weight equal to 75 to 80 percent of your 1RM repeatedly to failure, until you can no longer complete another repetition. During that last all-out effort repetition, the muscle is forced to contract all of its fibers. So at the point of momentary muscular failure, the maximum stimulus has been achieved, and your muscle will grow. Table 1.1 summarizes the load required for a range of repetitions based on the weight lifted during a 1RM.

TABLE 1.1

**Required Load
for Number of Repetitions**

Repetitions	Load (% of 1RM)
4	85
6	80
8	75
10	70

A hypertrophic training protocol consisting of six to eight repetitions to failure requires a load equivalent to 75 to 80 percent of your 1RM. Muscles grow most effectively when the maximum stimulus—muscular failure—is achieved within this rep range. Don't try to use the heaviest possible weight. Instead, select the heaviest weight you can control with perfect form. Concentrate on working one muscle unaided by momentum or the assistance of other body parts. Employ and maintain flawless form throughout the set—there's no place for compromise. Remember that it's the weight on the muscle that counts, not the weight on the bar.

Work Set

Perhaps the most controversial element of any training program is the optimal number of sets required to increase muscular hypertrophy. The debate concerns whether one set to failure is a sufficient stimulus to induce maximum hypertrophic adaptation or if multiple sets are required to elicit maximal muscular gains. According to the theory of general adaptation, muscular gains would plateau after the first set. But is this really the case?

Differences in training volume represent different degrees of stress to the neuromuscular system. Training volume is calculated as follows:

repetitions × sets × percentage of 1RM

When a muscle moves a weight, it performs work. In technical terms, the amount of work done depends on the size of the weight and the distance the weight is moved. You can make your muscles work harder by increasing the weight or increasing the distance moved by performing more repetitions or multiple sets.

No scientific evidence suggests that a greater training volume enhances strength or hypertrophy. There appears to be no significant difference in terms of muscular gains as a result of training with single versus multiple sets. Increases in muscle size and strength have been measured using single-set and multiple-set training; apparently, each method elicits similar neuromuscular adaptations. The question is which system represents the optimal amount of stress (volume) to induce maximal muscular adaptations? Strength increases will occur with the first set, but multiple sets may result in greater size gains. However, size and strength gains appear to follow the principle of diminished returns. With increases in training volume, the magnitude of adaptation may slow or diminish.

So can you really stimulate muscle hypertrophy with a single set to failure? In other words, can you walk into the gym, load up the bar with a weight equivalent to 80 percent of your 1RM, perform six reps to failure, and stimulate growth in every fiber of the muscle? The answer in practical terms is probably not. At the very least, you'd benefit from a warm-up set (or two) to get your muscle in the groove for that all-out maximal effort work set. In reality, you do need more than one set to recruit and exhaust all the fibers within a muscle. However, even though you perform a couple of sets to warm up to your maximum weight, it's only that final set to failure that really counts.

The *work set* is a single set of six to eight repetitions to failure using a load equivalent to 75 to 80 percent of your 1RM. The load must be heavy enough for momentary muscular failure to be reached within six to eight repetitions. It is this final all-out effort during the work set that generates muscle overload and elicits hypertrophy. The only purpose of lighter, warm-up sets in any given exercise is to prime your muscle to achieve one goal: a single all-out effort work set.

When you reach momentary muscular failure, squeezing out that last rep requires 100 percent intensity. But how can you be absolutely sure that *all* the muscle fibers have been recruited and that the muscle is totally exhausted? If you want to really annihilate the muscle, it's possible to go beyond failure and generate an even bigger hypertrophic response. Training beyond failure extends the work set into the zone of hyperintensity. This is an extreme stimulus that requires 110 percent effort. Even though the muscle has failed during the positive phase of the last rep, it is forced to perform more work. Later in this book, I'll describe 12 muscle-scorching steps to intensify your workouts (chapter 8).

To whet your appetite, here are three techniques to intensify your mass-building work set. First, when you hit failure during the positive (concentric) phase of the last rep, pause the weight in a static (isometric) contraction. Contract the muscle as hard as you can and hold the weight as long as you can until you reach failure in the static contraction. Then lower the weight as slowly as possible, forcing those muscle fibers to perform a final negative (eccentric) contraction. Finally, get a training partner to assist you in performing one last forced repetition. This brutal assault takes place after your muscle reaches the point of positive failure. The muscle then fails during the static contraction and fails again during the negative phase. This is what beyond-failure training is all about—the set begins when the muscle fails.

Make no mistake: These methods of extending the set beyond the point of failure are intense. When used effectively, they produce the ultimate trigger for hypertrophic adaptation and incredible mass gains. The static contraction, the negative rep, and the forced rep are brutal tricks to go beyond failure and induce muscular overload. To avoid injury when training with this degree of intensity, you must have a spotter, especially if you're using free weights.

Rest Interval

An important variable for generating an overload effect in multiple-set training programs is the amount of rest allowed between sets. Muscle fibers experience physiological change only if they are both recruited and exhausted. If too much time passes between sets, the exhausted muscle fibers might recover and be used in the next set, thus training the same group of muscle fibers over and over.

The theory behind multiple sets is this: As long as the time between sets is not sufficient for the muscle fibers to recover from exhaustion, a different group of fibers will be recruited and overloaded during the next set. In this way, the multiple-set method might overload more muscle fibers and elicit greater adaptations than a one-set protocol.

The rest interval between sets must be specific, not random. Resting no more than two minutes results in more muscle fibers being overloaded.

Compare this system to shooting a gun. You take precise aim, making sure to hit the target with each shot. You deliver all six bullets, exhausting the gun of its fire power. Then you reload as quickly as possible to deliver the next round. Each set goes boom, boom, boom, with maximum precision and intensity.

The time taken between sets has an important relation to workout intensity. Power is the rate at which work is done. The quicker the work

Time rest intervals carefully and don't go beyond two minutes between sets.

is performed, the more power is generated. In other words, your workout will be more intense when you complete it in less time. How much time you take to complete a workout naturally depends on the rest interval between sets. When your rest period is minimal, you complete the work in less time, and your workout is more intense. For a workout in which fat loss is a priority, shortening your rest interval is a useful way to burn more calories. An interval of 60 seconds or less allows just enough time to change the weight on the bar or relocate to the next exercise station.

Workout Time

Now we need to discuss the duration of your workout. This is based on your muscle's fuel tank—it is not an endless supply. Your muscle contains a store of chemical energy that is converted to mechanical energy. The muscle contracts, and movement occurs. Think of fuel stored in the gas tank of your vehicle. When burned, the chemical energy within gasoline is converted to mechanical energy. The wheels turn, and the vehicle moves along the road. When all the fuel is used up, the tank is empty, and your vehicle comes to a halt.

A similar process occurs inside your muscles. During exercise, your muscle's fuel tank begins to run low after 30 minutes; after an hour, it's empty. You are still able to exercise when your muscle's energy reserves are depleted because the muscle gets energy from other sources in your body. But at this point, your muscles shift into an endurance mode, such as being put on cruise control. The problem is that you can no longer accelerate, so you can't achieve maximum muscle stimulus. Your muscles are merely surviving, not growing. If you venture into muscle cruise control, it will take days for your muscle to refill its fuel tank. Muscle building is an anaerobic process. The training stimulus should be short and intense, not long and steady. Do what's necessary to trigger the hypertrophic response, then leave the gym, go home, rest, and grow.

For muscle growth, your workout time should not exceed one hour. Ideally, you should be in and out of the gym within 30 to 45 minutes. Remember that after an hour you have lost your power. You're out of ammunition and are shooting blanks. Get out of the gym before it's too late.

Recovery

If your goal is muscle growth, the time that elapses between workouts for a given muscle group or body part is important. An intense workout in which sets are performed to the point of muscle failure represents a massive insult, causing ultrastructural damage and protein degradation within the muscle tissue. This degree of stress is necessary for muscle hypertrophy. During recovery, protein synthesis occurs at an increased rate inside the muscle cells, which results in a size increase in the muscle fibers during the repair process. Scientific studies indicate that it takes five to seven days of complete rest to repair the muscle fiber disruption.

During the recovery phase, the muscle should not participate in heavy resistance exercise that directly targets the same body part. If the muscle's repair process is interrupted by another heavy workout, it will not achieve its maximum growth potential. The recovering muscle is, however, capable of assisting with workouts for other body parts and participating in low-resistance aerobic exercise.

To maximize muscle growth following an intense bout of hypertrophy training, the muscle should be rested for seven days. The ideal mass program should employ a split training system in which each muscle group is trained once each week. Divide your body into sections to create a series of workouts that you repeat over a weekly cycle.

Split training systems serve two valuable purposes. First, because the body is divided into sections, you get to focus all your efforts on a few selected muscle groups at each workout session. Second, even though you are performing several workouts per week, each individual muscle group is exercised only once every seven days, thereby allowing ample recovery time.

In this chapter you've learned the science behind muscle growth and how to manipulate the basic principles of weight training to create an intense workout. In the next chapter, we'll look at a technique for focusing your training to get the exact results you desire. You'll also learn how many exercises you need to do to shape each individual muscle and in what order you should do them.

FOCUSED CONTRACTION TRAINING

Focused contraction training (FCT) is an intelligent exercise system designed to generate the ultimate muscle-building stimulus. In FCT, every rep and every set of every workout serve a specific scientific purpose. Each exercise is hand-picked to build, shape, and sculpt your body. FCT requires you to train with your brain by engaging your mind first and then your muscle.

Central to FCT is the focused contraction technique, which has two key strategies. The first is that your mind must be completely focused on the muscle you are working; the exercise demands your undivided attention. Think of your muscle as an electrical appliance—plug it in and turn it on. The second strategy is that your muscle must be contracting during every phase of the repetition. Keep the muscle being worked under tension and don't let it relax at any time. Remember that it's time under tension that makes muscle grow. When you combine these two strategies, you get a focused contraction—the ultimate muscle-building formula.

The principles of FCT are as follows:

1. Work one muscle at a time.

2. Move one joint at a time.

3. Use one limb at a time.

4. Use a short, safe range of motion.

I'll explain how these principles work. The first three of them assist your ability to focus. The brain works best when it focuses on one task at a time. The more specific the task, the more attention the task receives from the brain. The ideal exercise to generate a focused contraction is one that works a single muscle by moving one joint of one limb—for example, the biceps flexing the elbow of one arm. When all other muscles and joints are taken out of the game, the mind–muscle link is enhanced, and you can focus all your effort on generating the maximum possible muscular contraction.

The fourth principle—use a short, safe range of motion—ensures a continuous muscular contraction throughout the phases of the repetition. To keep tension on the muscle during an exercise, the movement is restricted to a short range of motion. To illustrate this point, let's consider the biceps curl. As the weight is lowered and the elbow straightens, tension is temporarily removed from the biceps. When tension is off the muscle, it cannot generate an effective contraction. To prevent the biceps from taking a relaxation break at the bottom of the lift, stop 5 to 10 degrees short of full extension to retain tension on the muscle. Go ahead and feel the consistency of your biceps muscle contraction when your elbow is straight. Now compare it to when your elbow is bent. The muscle contraction is much harder with your elbow bent, isn't it? Because the biceps is at a mechanical disadvantage when the elbow is fully straight, it is prevented from contracting effectively. The same thing happens when your arms approach lockout during pressing movements. The tension is removed from the chest and deltoid muscles when the load switches over to the triceps. If you want to keep tension on the chest during bench presses and on the deltoid during shoulder presses, pause the repetition just short of the full lockout position.

Another aspect of this fourth principle is that a short range of motion is also a safe range of motion. At the extremes of joint movement, your anatomy is pushed to the limit. Your muscles, tendons, and joints are most vulnerable at the extremes of limb movement. In these positions, there is a higher risk of damage, particularly when lifting a weight. So a short, safe range of motion serves two purposes: It helps maintain a continuous muscular contraction, and it minimizes the risk of injury.

The principles of FCT do not apply to all exercises. But if the technique is incorporated into your workout, you will generate a focused muscle contraction. Before you apply these principles to individual exercises, we need to address a few questions: Which type of exercises should you choose? In what order should you perform the exercises? How many exercises are needed to shape each individual muscle?

EXERCISE TYPE

When you consider all the possible exercise variations—barbells, dumbbells, machines, cables, and so on—the list of choices is as fat as a small town's phone book. Way more exercises than you'll ever need. The bottom line is that there are two basic types of resistance exercise: isolation exercises and compound exercises.

As the name suggests, an isolation exercise isolates one muscle and typically involves motion at one joint. Examples include one-arm biceps curls, leg extensions, and shoulder raises. In contrast, a compound exercise requires the coordinated action of two or more muscle groups with motion occurring at more than one joint. Examples of this type of exercise include squats, bench presses, and shoulder presses.

By tradition, compound exercises are considered strength builders, and isolation exercises are favored for shaping muscles. To provide your muscles with the ideal stimulus, your exercise regime should include both types of exercise.

Now let's look at the sequence you should use in your workout.

A squat is a compound exercise.

EXERCISE ORDER

The order in which you perform your exercises can make a huge difference. To achieve the best muscular contraction, you'll need to focus your mind entirely on the muscle being worked. When this occurs, the muscle sends a message of approval back to your brain. This signal from the muscle back to the brain enhances the forward link from mind to muscle. In other words, your brain senses that the muscle is working and, in turn, is able to generate a more focused contraction. This is called the mind–muscle feedback loop. When you generate this positive feedback, your muscle can work harder, which results in greater muscular growth. If you can't sense the muscle contracting, you have no way of knowing if you're actually making it work. If that's the case, you're wasting your time on that exercise.

To help generate the mind–muscle feedback loop, my exercise regime prescribes an isolation exercise before a compound movement. I prefer to call the isolation movements primer exercises. The primer serves several purposes. First, it serves as a warm-up exercise to get the blood flowing through the muscle. Second, it makes it easy to develop the mind–muscle link right off the bat. Third, the muscle is primed and ready for the compound exercise. Finally, with the muscle already fatigued from the primer exercise, you don't need to lift so much weight during the compound exercise, which reduces the risk of injury associated with too heavy a weight.

When you group exercises for different body parts, remember to work from big to small. Train larger body parts such as the chest, quads, back, and shoulders before training smaller muscle groups such as the biceps, triceps, and calves. These smaller body parts function as support muscles for basic lifts such as bench presses, shoulder presses, rows, and squats. If you tire these smaller muscles first, they won't be able to assist effectively on the big exercises, which means the larger muscles won't get an adequate workout. Another benefit of training big to small is that the smaller muscle group will be warmed up and ready when its turn comes.

EXERCISE NUMBER

How many exercises does it take to shape each muscle group? The answer depends on the size of the muscle in question.

Smaller (limb) muscles such as the biceps and triceps attach to bone through thin, cordlike tendons. Because their narrow tendons attach to a single point on the bone, the biceps and triceps generate motion in one plane only—bending and straightening the elbow. All you need to do to effectively work the biceps or triceps is to perform a single movement. Biceps curls and triceps presses will effectively build those muscles, whether you use a barbell, dumbbell, or machine.

Larger (torso) muscles such as the deltoids, pectorals, and latissimus possess fanlike tendons that attach over a larger bony surface. These muscles are capable of generating movement in more than one direction. Thus, building these larger muscle groups requires a combination of exercises that work the muscle in several planes of motion.

To experience this type of fanlike tendon, examine the deltoid muscle of your shoulder. It's divided into three portions. In the front, the muscle attaches to your collar bone (clavicle). At the side, the lateral head attaches to the bone edge at the outer tip of your shoulder. Behind, the rear head attaches to your shoulder blade. Each part of the deltoid muscle serves its own function. The front deltoid raises your arm out in front of you. The lateral deltoid lifts your arm out to the side. The rear deltoid pulls your arm backward and behind. Feel each portion of the deltoid contract as you perform these three movements.

When a muscle such as the deltoid has multiple sites of attachment, it's not possible to target all aspects of the muscle with a single exercise. To build all three sections of the muscle, you need to do a combination of exercises that targets each portion of the muscle. Although the shoulder press might be considered the gold standard shoulder exercise, it works only the front portion of the muscle. You have to incorporate a side lateral raise and a rear deltoid exercise for proportioned deltoid development.

A proportionately developed muscle not only looks better but functions better too. Remember that the job of any muscle is to move a joint—the junction between two bones—and that each muscle that moves a given joint should be equally developed to optimize motion at that joint. It upsets the mechanics of a joint if one muscle is disproportionately stronger than its partner. Muscle balance is critical for proper joint function. For example, to optimize motion at the shoulder joint, all three heads of the deltoid muscle must be equally developed. This concept is of paramount importance when it comes to exercise selection.

The principle of muscle balance applies to all joints. Consider your elbow joint. Motion at this joint requires the coordinated action of the biceps muscle at the front and the triceps muscle behind. When the biceps muscle contracts, the elbow bends; when the triceps contracts, the elbow straightens. Each muscle causes motion in the opposite direction. The biceps is called the agonist muscle, and the triceps is called the antagonist. Another example of agonist and antagonist muscles are the quadriceps and hamstring muscles that straighten and bend the knee joint.

If the agonist muscle is stronger or weaker than its antagonist, the muscles become imbalanced. This upsets joint mechanics and thus increases the chance of injury. When constructing your exercise regime, be sure to select exercises that develop each muscle group equally and in proportion.

EXERCISE SELECTION

An effective bodybuilding program consists of a series of exercises that work all major muscle groups. For each individual muscle, there are only one or two basic movements. The chest muscles, for instance, can be worked with bench presses or chest flys. However, when you incorporate variation, the number of possible chest exercises becomes huge. Bench presses can be performed with the bench flat or tilted at an incline (head up) or a decline (head down) to work different areas of the pectoral muscle. The movement can be performed using a standard barbell, two dumbbells, or a machine. In other words, bench presses can be performed at three different angles using three different pieces of equipment. Do the math. The bench press has nine possible exercise variations. And that doesn't take into account the different types of machines, such as the Smith, Hammer, Nautilus, and so on.

Table 2.1 summarizes the different types of exercises for individual muscle groups. For variety, you have the choice (in most cases) of using free weights—barbell or dumbbells—or machines. The list includes exercises that I consider effective and safe when performed using the correct technique. I have excluded some exercises intentionally, either because I consider them biomechanically less effective or because they could do more harm than good. For example, upright rows and overhead triceps extensions place unnecessary stress on the shoulder joints. Dumbbell kickbacks will work the triceps, but there are better, more effective exercises to incorporate in your triceps workout. I have applied the same key principles of exercise efficacy and safety to all the exercise programs included in this book. I want you to get maximum results with minimum risk of injury.

▶ **Chest.** Now, you should not be performing nine variations of bench presses during your chest workout. That would be overkill. It's also a waste of time to duplicate the exact same exercise because this provides no additional benefit. Apply the principles described earlier. First, select an isolation-primer exercise, such as the chest fly, and a compound-strength exercise, such as the bench press. Then select a variation of each exercise to target different areas of the chest muscle. For example, perform chest flys on a flat bench to work the mid-chest. Then perform the pressing movement with the bench at an incline of 30 to 45 degrees to target the upper portion of the chest. If you want to add a third exercise, add a decline movement to work the lower chest. Get the idea? Whether you perform each exercise with free weights (barbell or dumbbells) or on a machine is a matter of personal preference and availability of equipment. Ideally, you should use a combination of free weights and machine exercises.

The same principles apply when selecting exercises for the shoulders and back. Because there are several different parts to these large muscles, choose exercises that target different regions of the muscle group.

▶ **Shoulders.** For the shoulder, use isolation movements, such as lateral deltoid raises, to work the outer (side) portion of the deltoid, combined with compound movements, such as shoulder presses, to target the front portion of the deltoid muscle. If you wish to add a third shoulder exercise, select rear deltoid flys to work the posterior (rear) section of the muscle. You can target the trapezius muscle with the shrug exercise, using a barbell, dumbbells, or machine.

▶ **Back.** For the back muscles, select an isolation exercise, such as an extension, for the lower back, then perform compound movements, such as chins, pulldowns, or rows, to work the upper back muscles. By changing your grip, hand spacing, or the angle of pull, you can target different regions of the upper back musculature. Wide-grip pulldowns or chins work the outer latissimus flare. Rowing exercises tend to add thickness to the inner (central) portion of the latissimus muscle. Pulling the weight toward your abdomen during rows targets

TABLE 2.1

Isolation and Compound Exercises for Specific Muscle Groups

Muscle group	Isolation exercises	Compound exercises
Chest	Chest flys using DB or machine. Flat bench targets the midchest, an incline bench targets the upper pecs, and a decline bench works the lower chest. Cable crossovers	Bench presses using BB, DB, or machine. Flat bench works the midchest, an incline bench works the upper chest, and a decline bench hits the lower pecs.
Shoulders	Deltoid raises using DB, machine, or cable Raise to the side for the lateral deltoid, to the rear for the posterior deltoid, and to the front for the anterior deltoid	Seated front shoulder presses, using BB, DB, or machine Trapezius shrugs using BB, DB, or machine
Back	Lower back extensions, flat or inclined Pullovers using DB or machine	Cable pulldowns Chin-ups Rows using BB, DB, or machine
Abdomen	Sit-ups, flat or decline Floor crunches Cable or machine crunches Twisting sit-ups/crunches for the obliques	Leg raises, performed hanging, on a decline, or using a machine
Quadriceps	Leg extensions (machine)	BB squats Machine squats (e.g., hacksquats) Leg presses
Hamstrings	Lying leg curls (machine) Standing leg curls (machine)	Straight-leg deadlifts, using BB or DB
Calves	Seated (bent-knee) calf raises	Standing calf raises Donkey (straight-leg) calf raises
Biceps	Preacher curls, using BB or DB Machine curls Concentration curls, using DB or cable	Standing biceps curls, using BB or DB Seated DB curls
Triceps	Cable triceps pushdowns, using bar or rope attachment Machine triceps pushdowns	Closed-grip BB bench presses Dips, using parallel bars or machine
Forearms	Wrist curls, using BB or DB Reverse wrist curls, using BB or DB	Reverse-grip BB biceps curls Hammer curls, with DB

BB = barbell; DB = dumbbell

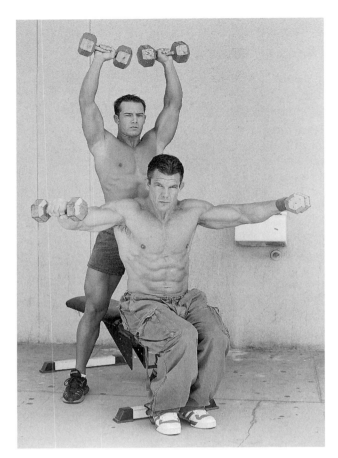

Combine an isolation movment, such as lateral deltoid raises, with a compound movement, such as shoulder presses.

the lower lats, whereas pulling the weight high toward the chest works the upper lats, lower trapezuis, and rhomboid muscles.

▶ **Abdomen.** Your waist is made up of two muscle groups: the rectus abdominals in the front and the obliques on each side. Sit-ups and crunches are isolation exercises that target the upper abdomen, and leg raises are compound movements that work the lower abdominals. If you incorporate a twisting motion, you'll work the oblique muscles too.

Selecting exercises for the limb muscles differs slightly from selecting exercises to work the muscles of the torso. The principles of isolation and compound exercises apply to the upper arm and thigh muscles, but the individual muscle groups are not subdivided into different target regions.

▶ **Legs.** To work the quadriceps muscle at the front of the thigh, combine leg extensions (an isolation exercise) with a compound exercise, such as squats or leg presses. The hamstring muscle at the back of the thigh can be built effectively using leg curls, an isolation exercise. Add compound straight-leg deadlifts if required, but remember that the hamstrings are also worked during compound quadriceps exercises, such as squats and leg presses. When it comes to working the calf muscle, there are two basic types of calf raises. One is done with the knees straight (standing calf raises, donkey calf raises) and the other with the knees bent (seated calf raises). The difference in effect between the two positions is negligible when it comes to developing the calf muscles. However, in the seated position, no stress is placed on the lower back. And, because the knees are fixed, motion occurs exclusively through the ankle joint, which makes seated calf raises an isolation exercise.

▶ **Arms.** Exercises for the biceps and triceps muscles of the upper arm also can be subdivided into isolation or compound movements. But because these muscles are smaller, they can be built effectively with one exercise each. I prefer isolation movements, such as preacher biceps curls and triceps pushdowns, using a machine or cable equipment. It's important to remember that the biceps is worked during compound exercises that target the back, and that the triceps is used in all pressing movements for the chest and shoulders. That's why I question the need for specific, additional compound exercises for the biceps and triceps. If you wish to strengthen your forearm muscles, there are two forms of isolation exercise. Wrist curls (flexion) performed with a barbell or dumbbell work the front or inner part of the forearm. Reverse wrist curls (extension) build the back or outer muscles. Don't forget that the forearm muscles are worked whenever you grip a bar. Consequently, the forearms experience a compound-type exercise during most upper body workouts.

PROGRAM PRESCRIPTION

The bodybuilding programs in this book describe in detail the workout regimes and nutrition plans necessary to build muscle and burn body fat. Each program serves its own purpose, and the programs are interchangeable depending on your needs. Your bodybuilding prescription must be individualized. By identifying three objectives, the FCT technique will guide you in selecting your personalized program.

▶ **Objective 1.** Focus on your primary goal. Your brain works best when it focuses on a single task. By choosing a specific target, you'll be slick and quick in cutting straight to the chase. To fine-tune your physique, identify exactly what your needs are. Do you want to gain muscle, torch body fat, or achieve both?

▶ **Objective 2.** Coordinate exercise and nutrition. Whether your quest is more muscle or less flab, you have two weapons at your disposal: exercise and diet. Exercise and diet are a tag team. They can function alone but work much better together. A low-calorie diet designed to shed body fat does not complement a mass-building exercise regime. For best results, combine exercise and nutrition in the most effective way.

▶ **Objective 3.** Tailor your exercise technique. The exercise protocol for maximizing muscle growth is different from the protocol for slicing off body fat. By manipulating the ground rules and tweaking your technique, you can create a program that does exactly what you want it to do.

In this chapter we've focused on selecting and combining the best bodybuilding exercises that stimulate muscle growth. However, the biological process of muscle hypertrophy won't occur unless you provide the necessary anabolic ingredients. Just as a plant needs sunshine and water to grow, your body has a list of demands that must be met. In the next chapter, you'll learn 12 steps to optimize your body's anabolic environment.

GAINING AN ANABOLIC ADVANTAGE

Anabolism is the process of tissue repair and growth. Your body must be in an anabolic state to build muscle. Intense exercise stimulates muscle growth, but that's only the spark that starts the anabolic process. The metamorphosis of muscle mass requires the right fuel intake, anabolic hormones, and a tincture of time. The anabolic process is just like cooking a meal—you put together the ingredients, turn up the heat, and wait.

You can take advantage of the anabolic state—that magical place where muscle is made—by following these 12 steps:

1. Be protein positive.
2. Facilitate carbohydrate construction.
3. Count on calories.
4. Add water.
5. Recharge to get large.
6. Use the anabolic window.

7. Make use of supplements for size.
8. Keep away from cardio.
9. Turn up testosterone.
10. Switch on growth hormone.
11. Put insulin to work.
12. Work your body type.

In this chapter, we'll look at each of these steps in more detail and incorporate them into the ultimate mass-building program.

BE PROTEIN POSITIVE

Proteins are the building blocks of body construction. You can't build a house without adequate raw materials, and you can't build muscle without protein. The amino acid components of protein are the bricks your body uses to repair and build muscle after exercise. Protein is rich in nitrogen, so high protein intake ensures a positive nitrogen balance. If your body is holding more nitrogen than it's excreting, it's in that magical anabolic state, and you're on track to add muscle mass.

To get your fill of amino acids, aim for 1 to 1.5 grams of protein per pound of body weight spread evenly over five to six meals per day. A 180-pound (81.6 kg) bodybuilder, for example, requires a minimum of 180 grams of protein a day, or 30 grams in each of six meals. Your intestinal tract is unable to absorb more than 50 grams of protein at once, so divide your daily intake over several meals. It you consume too much protein at one sitting, some of it won't be absorbed and will go to waste.

Foods high in protein include beef, poultry, fish, egg whites, milk, and whey. The easiest way to calculate your protein intake is to read the food label. As a rule of thumb, lean beef, chicken, turkey, and fish contain six to seven grams of protein per ounce. A large egg white contains six grams of protein, and milk contains one gram of protein per fluid ounce.

Consuming enough protein at regular intervals throughout the day ensures an adequate supply of amino acids and provides a positive nitrogen balance. This creates an anabolic stimulus, which activates protein synthesis for muscle building and leads to faster recovery. And if you want to be big, you have to be anabolic!

FACILITATE CARBOHYDRATE CONSTRUCTION

If protein is the brick of body construction, carbohydrates are the cement. These complex sugar molecules stimulate the release of insulin, a potent anabolic hormone that drives amino acids into muscle cells, where they are used for repair. Once your daily requirement of protein is met, carbohydrates generate weight gain.

Carbs are the body's preferred source of energy. After exercise, the body's storage tank of carbohydrates (muscle glycogen) depletes. When you eat plenty of carbs, these energy tanks fill up and encourage the body to hold onto protein to build new muscle. If you skimp on carbs, the tank empties quickly, forcing the body to burn protein for fuel instead of using it to repair muscle.

To add mass to your physique, you'll need to consume 1.5 to 2 grams of complex carbohydrates per pound of body weight each day. A bodybuilder weighing 180 pounds (81.6 kg) requires at least 270 grams per day, or 45 grams in each of six meals.

Quality sources of complex carbohydrates include potatoes, rice, pasta, yams, oatmeal, whole-wheat bread, and vegetables. To provide your body with the best anabolic environment for gaining muscle mass, partition your daily food intake in the ratio of 50 percent carbohydrates, 40 percent protein, and 10 percent fat.

COUNT ON CALORIES

To gain muscle, you must be in a positive caloric balance. The way your body uses the protein you eat is directly related to your calories. When your calorie intake remains slightly higher than your daily energy requirement, protein is used to build muscle. If your calorie intake is consistently low, your body burns fat and protein for energy. This works fine for losing body fat, but it's not the way to add muscle mass.

A good way to keep your calorie level adequate is to calculate your maintenance daily calorie requirement (your body weight in pounds multiplied by 10), then add an extra 10 percent of that value. For example, if you weigh 200 pounds (90.7 kg), your estimated maintenance daily intake is 2,000 calories. An additional 10 percent (200 calories) brings your daily calorie total to 2,200 calories. Add the extra 200 calories by consuming 50 more grams of carbohydrates.

Monitor your progress using a scale. If your weight isn't moving up after a week or two, you don't have enough calories to grow. Increase your calorie intake by another 5 percent each week until your weight starts climbing in the right direction. The gradual 5 percent increase in calorie consumption is to ensure your weight gain comes from adding new muscle and not from laying down body fat.

ADD WATER

Muscle is 70 percent water, so maintaining your body's hydration ensures maximum muscle cell volume and helps muscular growth. Failing to drink enough water can adversely affect your gains in muscle mass. When the body dehydrates,

Drink lots of water to keep your muscles hydrated.

water exits muscle cells, which sends the body into an antianabolic muscle-wasting state. A well-hydrated muscle is an anabolic muscle.

Begin hydrating your body first thing in the morning. Remember that an eight-hour overnight sleep is equivalent to one third of a day, during which time you consume no fluids. Drink at least half a liter of water upon waking. Caffeine drinks such as coffee and tea have a diuretic effect, squeezing water out of the body, so if you enjoy a caffeine fix—and that's okay—be sure to restock your fluid balance.

Under average environmental conditions, the body needs a gallon (nearly four liters) of water per day. In warmer climates, the daily water requirement increases to replace fluid lost through sweating. And although your work environment may be pleasantly cool during summer, air conditioning systems slowly dehydrate the body.

Keeping your body hydrated during exercise is essential. Water is all you need to replenish body fluids, provided your workout lasts under an hour. Sports drinks containing added electrolytes, such as sodium and potassium, are more beneficial to athletes who exercise for longer periods without eating. As long as you're in and out of the gym within an hour, there's no real advantage in consuming these formulated drinks during your workout.

RECHARGE TO GET LARGE

You need down time for muscle repair and recovery. You simply must get adequate rest if you want to grow. During exercise, muscle protein breaks down, and to restore protein balance, muscle protein synthesis is increased for at least 36 hours. Furthermore, to repair the muscle fiber disruption induced by a heavy weights session, the exhausted muscle requires five days of complete rest. Exercise-induced muscle growth is the ultimate result of the restoration of muscle protein balance and the repair of muscle tissue damage.

Rest days are a key component of any mass-building program. When your body is resting, it is building muscle tissue and restocking its energy stores. Without sufficient rest, your body remains in a catabolic state of negative protein balance and negative energy balance. If you deprive your body of the rest required for anabolism, your muscles won't gain size or strength. If you want to get large, you've got to recharge.

Another key requirement for anabolism is sleep. Do you know why babies sleep most of the time? Because they are growing. You need at least seven to eight hours of sleep each night if you want to optimize levels of your body's two most potent anabolic hormones—testosterone and growth hormone.

The best way to ensure an adequate and restful night's sleep is to develop a regular sleeping pattern. Go to bed every night at the same time, preferably eight hours before you have to wake up the next morning. With a regular sleep routine, your body becomes accustomed to a restful sleeping pattern. If you can't ensure at least seven to eight hours of sleep at night, try taking a 30- to 60-minute nap during the afternoon or early evening. Daytime napping is a good way to prevent chronic sleep deprivation.

Get plenty of rest to renew your energy and build your body.

USE THE ANABOLIC WINDOW

An anabolic window of opportunity opens immediately after you work out. Your body is drained of energy and in desperate need of refueling. After a workout, the body is a sponge for soaking up nutrients. This is a great opportunity to provide a quick burst of nutrients to jump-start the recuperation process.

A bout of heavy resistance exercise degrades muscle protein and depletes muscle glycogen. As part of the muscle's anabolic response to exercise, muscle protein synthesis and glycogen resynthesis begin immediately. The sooner you provide the necessary protein and carbohydrate building blocks, the quicker the muscle repairs the protein damage and restocks its glycogen energy store.

Research shows that if you consume protein and carbohydrates immediately after training, you can gain more muscle mass than if you wait an hour or two after the workout. To take advantage of that nutritional window of growth, you'll need quick-acting liquid nutrients rather than a solid meal that sits in your stomach for several hours. By the time a meal of solid food is digested, the anabolic window of opportunity has closed.

The best way to produce a potent anabolic effect is to drink a protein–carbohydrate supplement within 15 to 30 minutes of your workout. The best protein to use is whey (the quickest-acting bioavailable protein), which rapidly dissolves into amino acids, giving the body a quick fix of building blocks to expedite growth and recovery.

MAKE USE OF SUPPLEMENTS FOR SIZE

Nutritional supplements can be extremely helpful in your quest for muscle mass. In today's busy society, many people are at work or away from home at least eight hours a day. Under such circumstances, it's difficult to provide your muscles with a regular dose of quality nutrients in the right amounts. It's just not convenient to spend several hours in the kitchen each day preparing five or six muscle-building meals. Still, if you want those muscles to grow after all your hard work in the gym, you simply must meet their demands for fuel. And this is where quality nutritional supplements are useful.

The consumption of nutritional supplements following resistance exercise provides a hormonal environment that favors muscle anabolism. Some supplements provide extra nutrients to top off your dietary intake, whereas others are intended to stimulate muscle growth. Meal-replacement formulas are a convenient substitute for meals of solid food. Rather that resort to a fat-loaded meal of fast food, a high-protein and low-fat meal-replacement drink is a healthier and often cheaper alternative.

Protein is a key anabolic ingredient, but it's not easy to consume 1 to 1.5 grams of protein per pound of body weight each day from solid food, which often requires cooking. However, help is at hand in the form of quality supplements, such as whey protein. Low-carbohydrate protein supplements are available in powder forms, ready-to-drink bottles or cans, and tasty protein bars. With all the high-quality, convenient sources of protein out there today, it's easy to keep your protein tank full.

When sport supplements are scientifically compared, creatine comes out as the clear winner in terms of increasing muscle size and strength. This high-grade anabolic muscle fuel restocks energy stores, boosts muscle cell volume, switches on protein synthesis, and stimulates the release of growth hormone. When creatine is consumed with whey protein immediately after a workout, the muscle gains are superior to those obtained with either supplement taken alone. In other words, creatine and whey protein work as an anabolic tag team when used together after training.

The amino acid glutamine also has many benefits for those participating in intense exercise. Glutamine promotes muscle recovery, stimulates the synthesis of glycogen, and boosts immune function. Generally, a protein-rich diet should provide your body with a sufficient supply of glutamine. However, supplementing your diet with 5 to 10 milligrams a day provides extra insurance and prevents the muscle loss associated with glutamine deficiency.

KEEP AWAY FROM CARDIO

Exercise is a paradox of sorts. It is an insult to the body that triggers a stress response, inducing temporary catabolism. During this antianabolic state, body tissue breaks down. While short bursts of hardcore training stimulate new muscle growth, exercising too long and too hard causes an increase in the stress hormones cortisol, glucagon, and catecholamine. These catabolic hormones trigger the burning of glycogen and amino acids and cause the breakdown of muscle tissue.

If you want to live in an anabolic state and grow muscle, your workouts must be heavy and short. After an hour, you've lost your power and are entering a state of catabolism. Do only what is necessary to stimulate muscle hypertrophy, then get out of the gym and start the growth process. Step away from the stair machine, trot past the treadmill, and bypass the bike.

Aerobic exercise is great for improving overall health and promoting fat loss. But if your goal is to pack on muscle mass, then don't overdo your cardio. You won't gain weight if you're burning more calories than you're taking in.

Too much cardio hinders the bulking-up phase. If you're accustomed to playing basketball for an hour or so every day, you might need to change your habits a bit if you want to bulk up. It's fine to enjoy a short run or swim on the days you're not at the gym, but take into account the additional calories you've used. When you're trying to gain muscle mass, you always want to consume a surplus of calories.

TURN UP TESTOSTERONE

Testosterone is what makes men men. This male hormone boosts sex drive and builds muscle mass; it can make a difference in bed and at the gym. Testosterone is made in the testes; an adult male produces about 7 milligrams of testosterone each day, or almost 50 milligrams a week. The average level of testosterone for men is 500 nanograms per deciliter (ng/dl), although levels vary from 300 to 1,000 ng/dl, depending on age.

Men in their late teens and 20s have the highest peaks in testosterone levels, which means this is the optimal age for testosterone's anabolic effect. This doesn't mean that men over the age of 30 are significantly disadvantaged. In most men, the decline in testosterone level with age is a slow process; a plentiful supply remains for decades.

Testosterone has powerful anabolic actions that build muscle and reduce body fat. Testosterone

▶ increases lean muscle mass and bone density and cuts down on body fat,

▶ ensures a positive nitrogen balance by stimulating protein synthesis and improving protein utilization,

▶ enhances carbohydrate energy stores and promotes fat burning, and

▶ stimulates red blood cell production, which expands blood volume and improves oxygen delivery throughout the body.

There are ways to enhance testosterone naturally. Production of the hormone is stimulated by short bouts of intense exercise and at least seven to eight hours of sleep each night. Testosterone levels are optimized when protein intake is high (at least one gram per pound of body weight daily) and body fat is below 15 percent but not too low. Pro-hormone supplements containing steroid precursors such as androstenedione can also elevate testosterone. These measures—regular exercise, adequate sleep, high-protein diet, low body fat, and pro-hormone supplementation—won't increase your testosterone level above the normal range. The increases are small. However, small increases may be all you need to make a difference.

SWITCH ON GROWTH HORMONE

Growth hormone (GH) is a substance made naturally in the pituitary gland (located at the base of the brain). It's an anabolic hormone that stimulates growth of bone, cartilage, and other connective tissues, such as muscle. In fact, GH appears to affect the growth of just about every organ and tissue in the body. It promotes protein synthesis, nitrogen balance, amino acid uptake, and fat loss. It also has an anti-insulin effect in that it raises blood sugar.

Under normal circumstances, there is a nighttime peak in GH release about two hours after the onset of sleep. GH release is stimulated by several factors, including exercise, sleep, low blood sugar, creatine supplementation, and the amino acids arginine, lysine, ornithine, and tryptophan. Obesity blunts GH release.

Healthy aging in men is accompanied by a progressive reduction in the daily production of GH and testosterone. The age-associated decline in anabolic hormones begins at around 25 to 30 years of age and contributes to increased fat accumulation and diminished energy, strength, and muscle mass.

The average male body loses one pound (.45 kg) of muscle and gains one pound of fat every year after age 35. The good news is that you can minimize this age-related deterioration in your body by maximizing your anabolic drive using the strategies outlined in this chapter.

Heavy resistance exercise is a potent stimulus for increasing circulating anabolic hormones. You can also stimulate the release of GH by getting adequate sleep, keeping your body fat low, and avoiding sugar-loaded foods. Supplementing your diet with creatine and amino acids might be of additional benefit in boosting endogenous GH.

PUT INSULIN TO WORK

Two other important hormones involved in muscle growth and fat loss are insulin and glucagon. These hormones (produced in the pancreas) regulate carbohydrates and fat metabolism.

Insulin is released when blood sugar (glucose) levels rise following a meal of carbohydrates. The hormone transports glucose into cells, where it's used for energy or stored as glycogen. Simple sugars with a high glycemic index are absorbed quickly into the blood stream, causing a rapid release of insulin. This overproduction of insulin causes some of the carbohydrates to be deposited as fat instead of being stored as glycogen. Insulin is also involved in muscle growth because it transports amino acids into muscle cells. To facilitate this process, you need to consume carbohydrates. The key is eating the right kinds of complex carbohydrates in the right amounts.

Glucagon opposes the effect of insulin. Glucagon is released when blood sugar is low, typically several hours after a meal is eaten. In response to low blood sugar levels, glucagon converts stored glycogen into glucose. Because the body is running low on carbohydrates, glucagon also signals the body to start burning fat for energy. The ratio of insulin to glycogen in your body determines whether you'll gain or lose weight.

You can control this ratio by adjusting the relative proportions of protein and carbohydrates in your diet. Partition your food in a way to burn fat and build muscle. To gain muscular weight, you'll need a higher ratio of insulin. Thus, your daily nutrient intake should contain a higher proportion of carbohydrates than it does protein. Ensure that your nutrient ratio is about 50 to 60 percent carbohydrates, 30 to 40 percent protein, and 10 percent fat. Each meal should contain 30 to 40 grams of protein and 50 to 60 grams of carbohydrates, depending on your daily calorie allowance. Remember that once you've met your daily protein requirement—at least one gram of protein per pound of body weight—it's the extra carbohydrate load that packs on additional mass.

If you wish to lose body fat, you'll need a lower ratio of insulin. To increase glucagon and decrease insulin, eat slightly fewer carbohydrates and more protein. A simple rule of thumb is to adjust your protein-to-carbohydrates ratio to between 1 to 1 and 1.5 to 1. Partition your food so that the nutrient ratio is 50 to 60 percent protein, 30 to 40 percent carbohydrates, and 10 percent fat. One problem with reducing intake of carbohydrates is the decline in energy level, but minor adjustments on a day-to-day basis will tell you what works best in your case.

Don't take nutrient partitioning to extremes by going on a zero-carb diet in an attempt to lose more body fat. Under extreme low-carb conditions, muscular growth is virtually impossible because insulin levels are too low to transport amino acids into muscle cells. What's more, the body begins to break down its own protein—eating away at your muscles—in a desperate attempt to generate glucose for energy.

WORK YOUR BODY TYPE

We have different body types, just as we have different personalities. Your body is as individual as your fingerprint. The way you look is determined much more by your genes—the information contained in your body's cells—than by the jeans you're wearing.

The key to creating your own workout program lies in understanding body types and building a regime that accommodates your unique form rather than trying to change it. If you customize exercise and diet to your specific body type, you'll achieve a more effective transformation.

The three basic body types are ectomorph, mesomorph, and endomorph. The ectomorph is lean with a thin, delicate build that might have trouble gaining weight. The mesomorph is muscular with a hard, rectangular build that gains or loses weight easily. The endomorph is plump with a soft, round build that might have trouble losing weight.

Most people do not fit perfectly into any one category. Although one type usually predominates, most of us are a combination of body types. Because everyone's body is unique, body typing and workout design are not exact sciences. However, knowing your predominant body type helps in developing an ideal exercise and diet plan to meet your goals. Each body type requires a different bodybuilding prescription. The regime for an ectomorph differs from that for an endomorph because they are at opposite ends of the body-type spectrum.

The ectomorph body type tends to have a fast metabolism and has a tough time gaining muscle mass. The prime goal of an ectomorph is weight gain, so his bodybuilding program must be prescribed with this in mind. Exercise should focus on mass-building workouts, using heavier weights and fewer repetitions. Calorie-burning cardio should be kept to a bare minimum. An ectomorph's diet should contain a surplus of calories from complex carbohydrates to encourage anabolic weight gain.

The endomorph is the exact opposite. This body type tends to have a slow metabolism that stores unwanted extra calories. The endomorph easily gains weight but struggles to lose body fat. The main goal for an endomorph is burning off excess body fat. For his purposes, exercise should include several cardio sessions per week. Weight training should be performed at a fast pace with a higher range of reps. Diet is critical for the endomorph. To promote fat loss, daily calorie intake must be less than the daily calorie expenditure. The diet should be high in protein and low in fat, with a moderate amount of complex carbohydrates. Snacking and empty calories should be avoided.

The mesomorph body type is genetically advantaged when it comes to building lean muscle mass. Often, the mesomorph looks like an athlete even without training. This body type can benefit from almost any training protocol. However, to realize maximum potential, the mesomorph must build on his genetically gifted foundation. The mesomorph thrives on challenge and variation. This body type responds well to an alternating exercise program, switching between a bulking-up phase to pack on mass and a cutting-up phase to define the added muscle.

Now that you know how to heat up your anabolic furnace, you're ready to generate some serious muscle mass. In the next chapter we'll unveil your personal prescription for packing on pounds of muscle. Read on to discover an ultimate mass-generating workout and an advanced anabolic diet that induces dramatic surges in muscle size.

chapter

4

MASS GENERATOR PROGRAM

In the first three chapters we have looked at the science behind building muscle, learned the importance of exercise selection, and itemized the ingredients necessary for anabolic muscle growth. Now it's time to put these mass-building theories into practice.

If you're looking to pack on pounds of muscle fast, this is the plan for you. I have selected 14 of the best mass-building exercises and combined them into a three-day split workout routine that hits the muscles hard while providing ample time for recovery and growth. To optimize muscle hypertrophy, you'll perform between 6 and 10 repetitions, using 70 to 80 percent of your one-rep maximum (1RM) weight on each exercise. The mass-generating diet will deliver a surplus of calories to give your muscles the fuel they need to grow. You can expect to make significant muscular gains using this program; be sure to monitor and record your progress at regular intervals.

PROGRAM OVERVIEW

Workout Plan

As the name suggests, the mass generator program is designed to build muscle mass. To maximize muscle hypertrophy, the program emphasizes heavier weights and lower reps. Perform three sets of each exercise, using weights equal to 70, 75, and 80 percent of your 1RM. After an initial warm-up set of 10 reps, increase the weight on the second set so that your muscles fatigue after 8 reps. For the final "work" set, add more weight, and squeeze out 6 reps to failure. To make your muscles work hard, keep rest intervals as short as you can. Take 60 seconds of rest between the first two sets and 90 seconds before the final heavy set.

As you gain experience with this program, you can make the workout harder and even more effective by incorporating the high-intensity techniques described in chapter 8. Always take necessary safety precautions. To avoid accidents, use a spotter when lifting to complete muscular failure, especially when using free weights.

The mass generator workout routine uses a push-pull, three-way split-training system. I'll explain how it works. Session 1 involves upper body exercises (chest, shoulders, triceps) that require you to *push*. Session 2 is a leg workout that targets your quadriceps, hamstrings, and calf muscles. Session 3 involves upper body exercises (back, biceps) that require you to *pull*. This sequence groups together body parts that share similar exercise biomechanics. For example, in session 1, the *push* exercises for the chest also recruit the deltoid and triceps muscles. So, in effect, working the larger muscle group serves as a warm-up for working the smaller muscle groups, which follows later in the same workout. Similarly, in session 3, the *pull* exercises for the back muscles recruit and warm up the biceps. Thus, the smaller muscle is already pumped and ready for action when its turn comes. The leg muscles have session 2 all to themselves, working the largest muscle group (quadriceps) first in the sequence. The upper abdominals are worked with session 1 and the lower abs during session 3.

In this program, each muscle is exercised once every seven days. As you'll recall from chapter 1, your muscles need five to seven days to fully recover from an intense weights workout. Space the three workout sessions evenly during the week—for example, Monday, Wednesday, Friday. Perform your leg workout between the two upper body workouts; this allows more recovery time for those muscles that assist in both upper body sessions. Larger muscles such as the chest, shoulders, back, and quads are each assigned two exercises. Each exercise intentionally hits the muscle from a different angle. As a rule, an isolation exercise is used first, followed by a compound movement. Smaller muscles like the biceps, triceps, and calves are assigned one exercise each.

Three workouts per week might not sound like much exercise. However, during each 40-minute workout, you're required to work *hard*. If you want to build mass, you must push yourself. By the third set on each exercise, you should be lifting the heaviest possible weight for six reps to failure using flawless form. Then, with less than two minutes of rest, you're beginning the first set of the next exercise. Trust me, if you're putting all your effort into this mass-building routine, you won't want to work out more than three days a week! You'll soon realize that the four rest days per week provided during this program are an absolute requirement. Muscle grows when it's resting; recharge if you want to get large.

There's no calorie-burning cardio in the mass generator program. Your muscles will grow bigger and faster if you rest them completely between workouts. Thus, aerobic exercise is optional during your mass-building program. If you want to do some low-intensity cardiovascular exercise on the days you're not lifting weights, that's fine. But if you end up burning more calories than you're consuming, you won't gain muscular weight.

Nutrition Plan

To gain mass, you need to consume more calories than you burn. Those extra calories fuel muscle growth. So, how many calories should you consume each day during your mass-building program? Well, the first thing to do is calculate your maintenance daily calorie requirement (body weight in pounds multiplied by 10). Then add an additional 10 percent to this amount to get your daily calorie intake for mass-building purposes. In the end, you're providing your body with 10 percent more calories than it needs for energy production. The surplus calories are used to build muscle.

The next step is fun—you get to decide what food sources your calories come from. To promote muscular gains, the nutrient ratio of your diet should favor carbohydrates. I recommend partitioning your intake as follows: 50 percent carbs, 40 percent protein, and 10 percent fat. Once you've met your daily protein requirement for muscle growth (one gram of protein per pound of body weight per day), it's the extra carbohydrates that add muscle mass.

The 2,000-calorie sample meal plan (table 4.1) is a rough guide for someone who weighs 180 pounds (81.6 kg). The daily calorie intake is equivalent to an 1,800-calorie maintenance value plus 10 percent, which brings the calorie total to 1,980 calories. Remember that the daily calorie intake for gaining mass is determined by calculating your maintenance calorie requirement (body weight in pounds multiplied by 10) then adding 10 percent to this value. If your body weight is 180 pounds, your maintenance requirement is 180×10, or 1,800 calories per day. Since 10 percent of this figure is 180 calories, your daily intake should be 1,800 + 180, or 1,980 calories.

TABLE 4.1

Mass Generator Sample Meal Plan

Breakfast	Egg white scramble: Mix five egg whites and half a yolk with a tbsp of nonfat milk. Cook in a nonstick pan coated with a nonfat cooking spray. Serve on two pieces of whole-wheat toast. Drink one cup of black coffee or water. Calories: 350
Midmorning snack	Meal-replacement drink: Mix one sachet of a meal-replacement powder such as MESO-Tech (MuscleTech) with 12 oz cold water in a blender. Calories: 340
Lunch	Beef meal: Cook 6 oz of lean ground beef in a nonstick pan. Drain excess fat and water. Mix with steamed chopped carrots. Serve with one portion of pasta cooked in water and sprinkled with lemon juice and herbs. Drink a glass of ice water. Calories: 440
Midafternoon snack	Protein drink: Mix one serving protein powder such as NITRO-Tech (MuscleTech) with 4 oz water and 4 oz nonfat milk. Add one whole banana. Blend at high speed for 30 seconds. Calories: 240
Dinner	Chicken meal: Prepare a skinless chicken breast by squeezing lemon juice over it. Grill until cooked. Serve with a portion of steamed brown rice and broccoli. 1 tbsp of tomato ketchup is optional. Calories: 380
Late-evening snack	One serving of low-fat cereal or granola with 6 oz of skim milk Calories: 250
Daily values (approximate)	Protein: 200 g (800 cal), 40% Carbs: 250 g (1,000 cal), 50% Fat: 22 g (200 cal), 10% Total calories: 2,000

Adjusting the sample meal plan to your weight is easy. Remember that one gram of protein is four calories, one gram of carbohydrate is four calories, and one gram of fat is nine calories. Every 10 pounds (4.5 kg) in body weight is equivalent to 100 calories. Keeping the nutrient ratio at 40 percent protein and 50 percent carbohydrates, 100 calories equals 10 grams of protein (40 calories) plus 15 grams of carbohydrates (60 calories). To increase or decrease the calorie content to match your body weight, add or subtract these amounts from the sample meal plan.

Adjust your protein intake by changing the amount of protein powder added to your midafternoon snack or by changing the number of egg whites at breakfast (one egg white contains six grams of protein). Similarly, by adjusting the portions of pasta or rice at lunch and dinner, you can increase or decrease your intake of carbohydrates. But remember that the nutrition values in the sample meal plan are only approximate. Always check nutrition labels on the products you eat because values vary among brands. Supplementing your diet with creatine (chapter 10) will also help your mass-building efforts.

Adjust the content of the sample meal plan to match your individual body weight, using table 4.2.

TABLE 4.2

Daily Calorie Intake Based on Body Weight (Mass Generator)

Body weight (lbs)	Calories per day	Protein	Carbohydrates	Fat
220	2,400	240 g/960 cal	300 g/1,200 cal	26 g/240 cal
200	2,200	220 g/880 cal	275 g/1,100 cal	24 g/220 cal
180	2,000	200 g/800 cal	250 g/1,000 cal	22 g/200 cal
160	1,800	180 g/720 cal	225 g/900 cal	20 g/180 cal
140	1,600	160 g/640 cal	200 g/800 cal	18 g/160 cal

Nutrient ratio: 40% protein, 50% carbohydrates, 10% fat
Calorie value: 1 g protein = 4 calories; 1 g carbohydrates = 4 calories; 1 g fat = 9 calories
Daily calorie intake = (body weight in pounds $\times$ 10) + 10%

Progress Measurements

You'll be recording data in two categories: shape and function. In the first category, measure body weight using a scale; take body measurements—such as chest, arm, and thigh circumference—with a tape measure. In the second category, measure muscle strength by recording the maximum weight you can lift for six repetitions during the last set of each exercise. The stronger the muscle becomes, the bigger it grows. To continue growing, aim to increase the weight on each exercise by 5 percent every two weeks.

Results

After six weeks on this program, you should gain four to six pounds (1.8-2.7 kg) of muscle mass—as much as one pound (.45 kg) per week. Now this might not sound like a lot of muscle, but try taking a pound of ground beef and forming it in the shape of a pectoral muscle— you'll see that a pound of meat *is* substantial. Now imagine spreading six pounds of beef all over your body. That's a serious gain in muscular size. After six weeks on this mass program, you'll add an inch (2.5 cm) to your chest circumference and a half-inch (1.25 cm) to your arm and leg measurements. What's more, this extra muscle should boost your strength by 10 to 15 percent on every exercise.

So, enough talk already. Let's look at exercise techniques that forge a massive physique.

MASS GENERATOR WORKOUT

Mass Generator Exercise Program

Routine: Push-pull three-way split
Cycle: Three days per week
Schedule: Monday, Wednesday, Friday
Goal: Increase muscle mass
Detail: 3 sets of 10, 8, 6 reps
Rest interval: 60 to 90 seconds
Workout time: 40 minutes

PUSH MONDAY	
Chest	Dumbbell chest flys
	Incline bench presses
Shoulders	Dumbbell lateral raises
	Barbell shoulder presses
Triceps	Closed-grip bench presses
Abs	Decline sit-ups
LEGS WEDNESDAY	
Quadriceps	Leg extensions
	Barbell squats
Hamstrings	Lying leg curls
Calves	Standing calf raises

PULL FRIDAY	
Back	Chin-ups
	Barbell rows
Biceps	Barbell curls
Abs	Incline leg raises

PUSH (MONDAY)
Chest

DUMBBELL CHEST FLYS

Grab two dumbbells of equal weight and sit at the edge of a flat exercise bench. Lie back, keeping the dumbbells close to your chest. Stabilize your body by placing your feet flat on the floor. Push the dumbbells up into the start position with your palms turned toward each other (figure 4.1a). Begin the repetition by lowering the dumbbells out to the sides (figure 4.1b), bending your elbows slightly as the weights descend. Inhale as you lower the weight and feel your chest muscles stretch. Stop when your elbows reach bench level. Hold the weight for one second in the bottom position, then squeeze the dumbbells back up and together, exhaling as you lift. Keep your elbows slightly bent and your palms turned toward each other. Move the dumbbells in an arc, as if you're giving someone a bear hug. To keep the tension on the muscles, do not touch the dumbbells together at the top.

▶ **CHECK IT!** Don't let your arms go below the level of the bench; this places too much stress on your shoulder joint.

Chest flys also can be performed using machines with either a hand grip or elbow pads (page 140). Read the instructions printed on the machine for additional guidance.

Figure 4.1 Dumbbell chest flys: *(a)* hold dumbbells over your chest; *(b)* lower dumbbells to your sides.

Chest *(continued)*

INCLINE BENCH PRESSES

Lie back on an exercise bench tilted at an angle of 30 to 45 degrees (head up). Position your feet firmly on the floor. Take an overhand grip on the barbell with palms turned forward. Your hands should be slightly wider than shoulder-width apart. With your elbows locked straight, hold the bar in the start position above your chest (figure 4.2a). Begin the repetition by bending your elbows. Lower the weight slowly to the midpoint of your chest, just above the nipple line (figure 4.2b). Inhale as you lower the weight. Let the bar touch your chest, and hold it for one second. Do not let the bar rest on your chest. Without bouncing the barbell, push the weight vertically upward to the start position. Hold the bar with your elbows straight for one second. Repeat.

> ▸ **CHECK IT!** Remember that the bar travels vertically up and down perpendicular to the floor, not to your body.

You can also do this exercise using a Smith machine (see chapter 11).

Figure 4.2 Incline bench presses: *(a)* **hold the barbell over your chest;** *(b)* **lower the weight until the bar touches your chest.**

Shoulders

DUMBBELL LATERAL RAISES

Grab two dumbbells and stand upright with your feet about shoulder-width apart. Hold the dumbbells at arms' length just in front of your hips with palms turned toward each other (figure 4.3a). Raise your arms to your sides until they're level with your chin (figure 4.3b). Keep your palms

turned down and your elbows slightly bent during the lift. Your arms should move directly out to the sides until your elbows are level with your shoulders. Hold that position for one second, then lower the weight slowly back to the start position. Keep your torso upright during the movement. A slight forward tilt is acceptable, but don't lean backward.

You can also do this exercise while seated using dumbbells (page 85) or with one arm at a time using a cable attached to a low pulley (page 163).

▸ **CHECK IT!** Don't raise the dumbbells too high because this places undue stress on the shoulder joints. Your hands should be level with your chin, elbows just below shoulder height.

Figure 4.3 Dumbbell lateral raises: *(a)* hold dumbbells in front of hips; *(b)* lift weights to the sides.

Shoulders *(continued)*

BARBELL SHOULDER PRESSES

Sit on a bench with the backrest upright at a vertical angle. If the backrest is adjustable, tilt it back about 20 degrees to optimize body position. Firmly position your feet on the floor and lean back onto the bench. Take a shoulder-width grip on the barbell with palms turned forward. Remove the barbell from the rack; position it overhead with elbows locked (figure 4.4a). From the start position, lower the weight slowly in front of your face until it touches your collar bone (figure 4.4b). Pause for one second, but don't allow the bar to rest on your upper chest. Push the bar vertically up until your arms are fully extended overhead. Pause for one second and repeat.

▸ **CHECK IT!** Avoid behind-the-neck shoulder presses because they can be trouble for your shoulder joints. Keep your hands in front where you can see them. Don't allow the weight to stray back and forth during the movement.

You can perform this exercise using dumbbells with palms turned forward or use a seated front press machine.

Figure 4.4 Barbell shoulder presses: *(a)* **hold the barbell overhead;** *(b)* **lower the weight to your chest.**

Triceps

CLOSED-GRIP BENCH PRESSES

Lie supine on a flat bench; grab the bar with an overhand grip, hands about four to six inches apart. In the start position, the bar is held fully extended over your chest (figure 4.5a). Lower the barbell slowly in a vertical plane until it touches your lower chest (figure 4.5b). Keep your elbows close to your sides as the weight is lowered. Pause momentarily at the bottom, then press the bar upward until your elbows are fully extended. Squeeze the triceps for a count of one, then repeat.

▶ **CHECK IT!** Keep your buttocks in contact with the bench throughout the movement.

Figure 4.5 Closed-grip bench presses: *(a)* hold the barbell over your chest; *(b)* lower the weight until the bar touches your chest.

Abs

DECLINE SIT-UPS

Adjust a decline bench to a 20-degree angle in relation to the floor (head down). Hook your feet under the roller pad and rest the back of your legs on the knee pad. Initially, sit upright on the bench so that your abdomen almost touches your thighs. Your hands can be held together behind your lower back or interlocked behind your head (figure 4.6). Begin the exercise by lowering your torso slowly backward while contracting your abs. Go back about a foot until your torso is almost parallel to the floor. Holding the bottom position, flex those abdominal muscles for one second. Crunch back to the start position, bending at the waist. In the top position, your body should be perpendicular to the floor but not touching your thighs. Hold in the contracted position for one count, then repeat.

This is a great exercise for the upper and middle abdominal muscles. As you gain strength, you can increase the number of reps, tilt the bench at a steeper angle, or hold a small weight plate on your chest.

▶ **CHECK IT!** Don't go back too far. When tension is released from the abdominals, stress is placed on the lower back.

Figure 4.6 Sit upright on the bench.

LEGS (WEDNESDAY)
Quadriceps

LEG EXTENSIONS

Sit at a leg extension machine. Adjust the backrest so that the backs of your knees fit snugly against the seat and your thighs are supported. Position your ankles under the roller pad. If the pad is adjustable, position it so it rests just above your ankles on the lowest part of your shins (figure 4.7a). Grip the handles on the machine for support. From the start position, contract your quadriceps to straighten your knees (figure 4.7b). Lift the weight all the way up until your knees are straight. Pause for one second at the top, making sure to flex your quadriceps. Lower the weight slowly until your knees are bent 90 degrees. Hold the weight momentarily in the bottom position, then repeat.

► **CHECK IT!** Don't let your hips rise off the seat.

Figure 4.7 Leg extensions: *(a)* **sit in leg extension machine;** *(b)* **straighten legs.**

47

Quadriceps *(continued)*

BARBELL SQUATS

Position an empty barbell onto the squat rack, level with your upper chest. Load equal weight plates on either side of the bar and secure them with safety collars. Note the center of the bar and grip the bar in an evenly spaced overhand grip, hands slightly wider than shoulder-width apart. Step under the bar and position it comfortably on the upper portion of your back. Lift the bar off the rack and carefully take one step away from the rack. Position your feet in line with your hips and point your toes slightly outward. This is the start position (figure 4.8a). Begin the repetition by bending your knees and slowly lowering your hips straight down until your thighs are parallel to the floor (figure 4.8b). During the movement, be sure to keep your back straight, your chin up, and your grip firm to stabilize the bar on your shoulders. Don't lean too far forward because this places more stress on your lower back, and you might lose your balance. Once you reach the bottom position, push the weight up using

your thighs and hips until your knees are straight. Inhale deeply during the descent and exhale on the way up.

If you have trouble balancing during this exercise, place a one-inch thick wooden block under your heels. The squat is a great leg exercise, but it's also very demanding, requiring your full attention. Errors in technique can cause injury to your lower back or knees.

> ▶ **CHECK IT!** Avoid squatting below parallel position; this can damage your knees.

Figure 4.8 Barbell squats: *(a)* stand with the bar across your shoulders; *(b)* lower your body until your thighs are parallel to the floor.

Hamstrings

LYING LEG CURLS

Lie facedown on a leg curl machine and position the back of your ankles under the roller pads (figure 4.9a). Grip the handles for support. From the start position, curl the weight up by bending your knees (figure 4.9b). Bring your heels toward your buttocks. When the roller pad touches the back of your hamstrings, hold the contracted position for one second. Slowly lower the weight back to the start position with your legs almost straight. Hold at the bottom momentarily and repeat.

> ► **CHECK IT!** Don't lift your hips off the machine.

You can also do this exercise using an upright leg curl machine, working one leg at a time (page 95).

Figure 4.9 Lying leg curls: *(a)* **lie on a leg curl machine;** *(b)* **bring heels toward buttocks.**

Calves

STANDING CALF RAISES

Place the balls of your feet on the platform of a standing calf raise machine. Position your shoulders under the pads and stand upright with your knees straight. Your feet should be directly beneath your hips. Slowly lower your heels as far as possible, stretching your calf muscles (figure 4.10a). Keep your back straight and don't bend your knees. Hold the stretch in the lower position for one second. Lift the weight by raising your heels as high as you can (figure 4.10b). At the top position, contract your calf muscles hard and hold for one count. Lower the weight back slowly and repeat.

▶ **CHECK IT!** Don't let your back hunch; keep your knees straight.

Variations of straight-leg calf raises are described in chapters 7 and 11.

Figure 4.10 Standing calf raises: *(a)* **lower your heels;** *(b)* **lift the weight by raising your heels as high as possible.**

PULL (FRIDAY)
Back

CHIN-UPS

Grasp an overhead bar with an overhand grip, hands slightly wider than shoulder-width apart. Hang at arms' length, then lift your feet off the floor so that your body weight is suspended from your arms (figure 4.11a). Bend your knees slightly and lock one foot over the other, behind the plane of your body. From the start position, pull your body slowly upward until your chin touches the bar (figure 4.11b). Think of your hands as hooks. Make your upper back muscles do the work, pulling your elbows down and back as your torso ascends. Pause briefly at the top, squeezing your latissimus muscles. Then slowly lower back down to the start position.

If you find chin-ups too difficult, or too easy, substitute this exercise with wide-grip pulldowns (chapter 7).

▸ **CHECK IT!** Don't bounce or jerk. Keep your knees pointing toward the floor throughout the movement.

Figure 4.11 Chin-ups: *(a)* hang at arms' length; *(b)* pull upward until your chin touches the bar.

Back *(continued)*

BARBELL ROWS

Stand with feet about hip-width apart. Pick up a barbell with a shoulder-width grip. Tilt your upper body forward at the waist, making a 45-degree angle to the floor (figure 4.12a). Keep your lower back straight and head up. Begin the repetition by pulling the bar upward until it touches your upper abdomen (figure 4.12b). Pause briefly at the top, contracting your back muscles. Slowly return the weight to the straight-arm start position. This exercise can be performed with an overhand (palms turned down) or underhand reverse grip (palms turned up).

► **CHECK IT!** Don't hunch or round your lower spine; avoid jerking up with your body.

Variations of the row exercise, such as seated rows (chapter 7) and dumbbell rows (chapter 11), are less strenuous on the lower back.

Figure 4.12 Barbell rows: *(a)* **grip the barbell, torso angled to the floor;** *(b)* **lift the weight to your upper abdomen.**

Biceps

BARBELL CURLS

Stand upright holding a barbell at arms' length in front of you (figure 4.13a). Your hands should be shoulder-width apart in an underhand (palms up) grip. Curl the weight up by bending your arms at the elbows (figure 4.13b). Keep your elbows at your sides and your back straight. There should be little, if any, movement at the shoulder. Pause for one second at the top of the lift, keeping the bar at chin level. Lower the bar slowly to start position. Pause momentarily at the bottom of the lift, then repeat.

To keep tension on the biceps, stop a few degrees short of full elbow extension at the bottom and don't let the bar rest on your upper thighs. There should be no backward or forward motion of your torso.

You can also do this exercise on a biceps curl machine.

> ▸ **CHECK IT!** To reduce stress at the wrists and elbows, avoid narrow or wide grips on the bar.

Figure 4.13 Barbell curls: *(a)* stand holding the barbell; *(b)* curl the weight.

Abs

INCLINE LEG RAISES

Adjust an abdominal bench to a 30-degree angle in relation to the floor. Lie supine with your head uppermost. Hold the bench behind your head to stabilize your torso (figure 4.14a). From the start position, raise your legs at the hips. As you pull your thighs toward your chest, keep your knees slightly bent and your legs together. Tighten your lower abdominals as your hips bend. Stop before your thighs touch your chest and hold the contracted position for one second (figure 4.14b). Then slowly lower your legs under control. Stop before your heels contact the bench (or the ground) to keep tension on the abdominal muscles. Hold in the bottom position momentarily, then repeat.

▶ **CHECK IT!** Position the bench at a steeper incline to increase the resistance.

You can also do leg raises while lying supine on a flat exercise bench. Variations of this exercise are described in chapters 7 and 11.

Figure 4.14 Incline leg raises: *(a)* **lie back on an incline bench;** *(b)* **lift legs toward chest.**

PART II

CUTTING BODY FAT

chapter 5

LEAN MUSCLE TRAINING

Building your muscles is one thing; being able to see them is another. What's the point in owning a set of strong, shapely muscles if you can't see them? It's like having a mint-condition vintage car that never leaves the garage. In the space between your skin and the underlying muscle lies a layer of fat. Fat owns that space; we rent it. Unless your body fat percentage is below 10 percent, that insulating layer of lard will obscure your hard-earned muscle mass.

The human body contains 20 to 30 billion fat cells. As well as providing a layer of insulation from the cold, body fat serves as an energy savings account; instead of money, the currency in this account is calories. The more calories you feed into the bank, the bigger the account gets.

Fat is a potent source of energy. Each gram of fat contains nine calories, compared to four calories per gram of protein or carbohydrates. So it's understandable that our bodies prefer to invest energy funds in a fat account. Fat storage is a survival mechanism; the swollen fat cells provide a savings account of calories to draw on during lean times. Fat cells are also resilient—they love to stick around and hate to get too small.

Not all fat is the same. A fat cell's precise qualities vary according to which fat deposit in the body it resides in. Fat from the belly, for instance, will lose and gain lipid more quickly than fat from the thighs and buttocks. When you're ridding your body of lard, the thighs and buttocks are the last areas that shed fat. In many people, these stubborn fat deposits won't disappear until body fat percentage slides below 6 percent.

So, how do you get rid of body fat and deflate that spare tire of blubber? You must stop feeding excess calories into the savings account. Stop making deposits and start making withdrawals. When you withdraw calories from the savings account, the fat cells shrink in size, and their number decreases.

In the fight against flab, the points on the scorecard are calories. Calories are the units of energy contained in food and are a measure of how much energy your body uses. When you consume more calories each day than you actually need, the excess is put into storage, and your body fat savings account grows. On the other hand, if you don't consume enough calories each day, the deficit is taken from savings—you burn body fat to provide the extra energy.

Each pound of body fat contains 3,500 calories. If your average daily calorie intake is 2,000 calories, you'd have to starve yourself for two days to lose that pound of fatty flesh. Even if you starved yourself for a week, you'd lose only four pounds of body fat.

Starving out the army of fat cells is a tough battle to win. The good news is that we have a secret weapon—exercise. Exercise requires energy. To provide this energy, your body taps into its fat reserves. Exercise forces fat cells to give up their ammunition, their calorie stores. As the fat cells lose lipid, they shrink in size and decrease in number.

Remember that losing fat depends on the balance between calories consumed and calories used. To kill off the fat cells, you either consume fewer calories, burn more calories, or both. As the fat melts away, your muscles come out to play, visible for all to see.

CALORIE-CRUNCHING TACTICS

The exercise of choice in the fight against fat is called aerobic or cardiovascular (cardio) exercise. The term aerobic indicates that the process requires oxygen. Aerobic exercise requires continuous movement with minimal resistance to stimulate the heart and lungs and expend calories—in other words, a cardiovascular endurance exercise. These terms are used to describe low-intensity, long-duration exercises such as walking, jogging, and cycling.

In building an effective aerobic program, you need to address several questions. How long should the activity last? How hard should you work? Which type of exercise is best? How many calories will you burn? How often should the activity be performed? When's the best time to do cardio? Let's discuss these questions in turn.

The duration of the exercise is important. To get an adequate training effect from aerobic activity, at least 20 to 30 minutes of continuous exercise is required. This is the minimum amount of time you should spend on cardio. If you want to maintain muscle size, don't exceed 60 minutes of cardio exercise. Longer periods of exercise are an endurance challenge, and your muscle framework will evolve into that of an endurance athlete. For fat burning, regular short bursts of cardio are superior to infrequent bouts of extended duration.

As a rule, the intensity of the cardio exercise (how hard you work) should be as high as you can make it. In other words, work as hard as you can for the 30-minute period. The harder you work, the more calories you burn. It's a mistake to assume that your half-hour of cardio is a casual stroll. If you're not breathing heavy or breaking into a sweat, you're probably not working hard enough. You can tell the people who are exercising hard during cardio—they're not reading or talking!

If you have trouble judging your intensity level, here is a calculation that might help. Calculate your maximum heart rate by subtracting your age from 220. Multiply this figure by 0.7. With this number, find your target heart rate, which is 70 percent of the maximum heart rate for

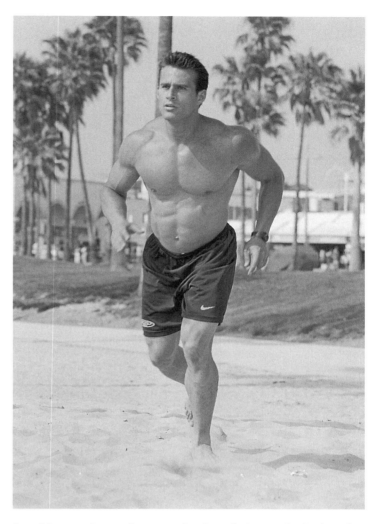

Aerobic exercise such as running is a vital part of a fat-burning program.

someone your age. For example, the target heart rate for a 30-year-old would be 133 (220 − 30 = 190; 190 × 0.7 = 133). This means that the target heart rate for a 30-year-old engaging in cardio activity is at least 130 beats per minute (70 percent of the estimated maximum heart rate of 190 beats per minute). Monitor your heart rate by feeling the pulse at your wrist and timing it over one minute using a watch. Eventually, you'll get to know how hard you should work to achieve your target heart rate without needing to constantly check it. Many cardio machines have built-in heart rate monitors. You also can note the speed gauge. For example, 100 rpm on the stationary bike should put your heart rate in the target range. The worse case scenario is that you become so obsessed with checking your pulse that you're not paying enough attention to the exercise.

When it comes to choosing a cardio exercise, personal preference is the key factor. There is a range of different types to chose from. Outdoor activities include walking, jogging, and cycling. Indoor activities include riding a stationary bike, running on a treadmill, walking on a stair climber or elliptical trainer, or swimming in the pool. You're more likely to do the exercise effectively and regularly if you enjoy the activity. If you like variety, try different activities on different days of the week.

What determines how many calories you burn? The larger you are and the harder you work, the more calories you burn. Many factors play a part, such as your size, effort, muscles involved, fitness, amount of body fat, movement efficiency, and environmental conditions such as weather. With all these influences, accurately predicting how many calories you burn during your activities can be tough. However, you can make a useful approximation based on body weight. To help with your exercise program, have a look at the calorie-burning chart I've compiled for you (table 5.1).

Using the chart is easy. Let's say you weigh 200 pounds (90.7 kg). The approximate number of calories burned during one hour of weight training would be 200 × 2.0, or 400 calories. The calories burned during a 30-minute weight-training session would be 200. For comparison, 30 minutes of walking would burn 240 calories, cycling would burn 280 calories, and jogging would burn 420 calories. The calorie expenditure using most cardio machines is similar, so personal preference is probably the way to go. Remember that these figures are only estimates, but it's always true that the harder you work, the more calories you burn. An intense half hour of weights in which you lift as much weight as possible with minimum rest between sets will burn more than the estimated value. The key to burning more calories during a weight-training session is reducing the rest interval between sets and exercises.

TABLE 5.1

Calorie Burning Chart

Activity	Calories*
Jogging (6 mph)	4.2
Jumping rope	3.8
Swimming	3.5
Cycling (10 mph)	2.8
In-line skating	2.6
Walking (3 mph)	2.4
Weight training	2.0

*Multiply this number by your body weight in pounds to calculate the calories burned per hour.

If you'd prefer to make a quicker calculation of the number of calories burned, use these estimates for one minute of exercise:

▶ **Running:** 12 calories per minute
▶ **Cycling:** 8 calories per minute
▶ **Walking:** 6 calories per minute
▶ **Weight training:** 6 calories per minute

Remember that this minute-by-minute estimation does not take into account your body weight. In fact, for every pound of lean muscle you pack onto your frame, you'll burn an additional 30 calories per day at rest.

Aerobic exercise should be done two to three days per week, preferably on the days you don't train with weights. Cardio and weight training serve different purposes. With weight training, you're aiming to grow muscle size and strength. During cardio, you're trying to expend calories to burn fat. When you combine cardio and weight training in the same workout, you'll still burn fat, but muscle growth might suffer. Personally, I like to alternate between a weight-training workout one day and a cardio session the next. If you prefer to combine the two types of exercise during one workout, do the weights session before the cardio.

The fat-burning effect of cardio is greatest if you perform the exercise first thing in the morning on an empty stomach. Since you have fasted or starved for eight hours overnight, your body's supply of glucose energy is low. As a result, you're more likely to tap into fat reserves for energy. Whatever time of day you perform cardio, you can still achieve a similar effect by not eating for at least two hours before exercise. Furthermore, your body continues to burn stored energy even after you stop exercising. To maximize this effect, wait an hour after cardio before eating. Remember that the goal of low-intensity, calorie-crunching cardio is to lose body fat, not to generate an anabolic effect.

When it comes to choosing your own personal exercise prescription, be guided by your individual body type and goals. If you are an ectomorph, your primary goal is to gain muscle mass. Your particular focus lies with weight training rather than cardio, and you should select the mass generator program discussed in chapter 4. On the other hand, an endomorph needs to focus on fat loss. For this purpose, you'll need to include some calorie-crunching cardio; you should select the body fat blitz program covered in chapter 7.

SIX-PACK SECRETS

During my many years as a fitness magazine columnist, the question I'm most frequently asked is, "How do I get a six-pack?" Everybody wants a set of defined abdominal muscles. The trouble is that the misconceptions surrounding how to attain a tight midsection leave many people struggling to find methods that work. You see, you can perform as many sit-ups as you like or work on crunches until you're blue in the face, but until you ditch that spare tire around your waist, you'll never see a chiseled set of abs, period. If you want abs that look like they were etched out of stone, you have to carve off the fat that covers them.

There is no simple "ab-solution," and there isn't a magic pill, but I do have a six-pack prescription for phenomenal abdominals. The process consists of several simple steps that, when combined, work like magic.

   1. **Do your cardio.** Perform 30 minutes of cardio at least three times a week. During each session, you'll burn around 200 calories. What's more, if you do your cardio first thing in the morning on an empty stomach, you'll burn up to three times

Follow the steps to "ab-solute" perfection.

more fat. Because you haven't eaten all night, your sugar levels are low, which makes early morning the optimal time for fat loss. When you perform cardio in this state, your fat stores are used as fuel.

2. **Eat six small meals a day.** If you eat smaller meals, your stomach can reduce in size, and you'll feel satisfied with less food. This helps prevent that bloated belly look. Consuming smaller meals every three hours provides a constant supply of energy and prevents hunger pangs.

3. **Reduce your calorie intake.** If you burn more calories each day than you consume, you'll lose body fat. The best way to reduce calorie intake is to cut down your consumption of dietary fats. Each gram of fat contains nine calories, which is double the amount contained in either a gram of protein or carbohydrate. Be sure to stick with low-fat or nonfat food products.

4. **Increase your protein intake.** Protein is less likely to cause body fat deposits than either carbohydrates or fat. The larger the protein component of your diet, the more effective your powers of fat burning. Consume one gram of protein per pound of body weight daily to feed your muscles and keep your metabolism elevated.

5. **Cut back on carbohydrates.** Dietary carbohydrates are essential for energy, but eating more carbs than you need will feed your body fat. When your carbohydrate stores are filled, excess sugar is converted to fat. If you restrict your carbohydrate intake, your body is forced to burn fat stores for energy. To achieve this effect, carbohydrates should account for less than 50 percent of your total calorie intake each day. When choosing a carbohydrate, pick those with a low glycemic index, such as the complex carbohydrates in rice, potatoes, and pasta. Keep your consumption of low glycemic simple sugars, such as fruit, to a minimum.

6. **Drink water, not soda.** For health reasons, it's important to keep your body well hydrated. But if you satisfy your thirst with soda, milk, fruit juice, or alcohol, you're consuming extra calories. It's easy to forget that an eight-ounce beverage can contain 100 to 200 calories. If you want to keep the fat off, water is the way to go. Consume at least one gallon of water per day.

7. **Work your abdominals.** Everybody has abdominal muscles. The problem is that they hide under a layer of body fat. Targeting your waist with specific abdominal exercises is important if you want a six-pack. Still, as I've mentioned, it doesn't matter how many exercises you do if your abdominals are covered in fat because no one is going to see them. In fact, your body fat percentage must be below 10 percent before you'll witness any visible benefit from abdominal exercises. But even if you can't see the individual muscles, a toned and tight abdomen prevents your belly from protruding. Choose a series of exercises that work all areas of the abdomen. Sit-ups or crunches target the upper abodominals, leg raises work the lower abdominals, and a twisting exercise tones the obliques. Perform three sets of each exercise two or three times each week.

8. The more lean muscle you have, the more calories you'll burn on a daily basis. For every pound of lean muscle you add, you'll burn an extra 30 calories per day at rest. As you know, more calories burned equals more fat lost.

9. Try a fat burner. A potent fat loss supplement containing the ephedrine, caffeine, and aspirin (ECA) stack can accelerate fat loss. Via a process called thermogenesis, the ECA stack elevates your body's metabolic rate, so you burn more calories. Make sure you read the product label carefully, and if you have any medical conditions, check with your doctor before using fat loss supplements. For more information on fat burners, see chapter 10.

10. Be dedicated. You won't get a six-pack overnight. If you follow all the steps, you can lose a pound or two of body fat each week, and within a month you'll witness progress. There's no substitute for dedication and discipline. Be patient, stick with the plan, and soon you'll have your very own six-pack.

The most important exercise to develop a slim waist is cardio, but what you eat is equally important. If you have another look at the 10 steps, you'll see that 5 of them involve changes to your diet. So, in addition to burning calories, you must address calorie consumption which brings us to the next item on the agenda. Yes, you've guessed it—diet. Next chapter, please.

HARD MUSCLE FUEL

It's true that we are what we eat. The problem is we eat too much. Food, glorious food, anytime, anywhere. Eating is so convenient that it's hard to resist gulping down more calories than we need. Please, sir, I want some more. Breakfast, brunch, lunch, then a munch on some snacks, followed by an appetizer, dinner, dessert, and around bedtime, a midnight snack. It seems that during every waking hour, we're satisfying our cravings for delicious treats that dance on our taste buds.

Whereas the key factor in generating muscle mass is exercise, the secret ingredient in fat loss is diet. In other words, you can't build muscle unless you exercise. Even if you eat all those fancy supplements, your muscles won't grow if you don't exercise. On the other hand, nutrition plays the biggest role in losing body fat. With the right diet, you can lose weight, with or without exercise.

When it comes to providing fuel for your body, quality overrules quantity. You should be running on premium gasoline. Your body works much better on the good stuff. If you want to build muscle and stay lean, proper nutrition is crucial.

But for many people, getting proper nutrition means dieting, and for some people dieting conjures up anxiety, fear, and loathing. One thing you'll be happy to hear is that my fuel prescription does not focus on food restriction. We pay more attention to other details, such as choice, preparation, and timing. You'll get to eat, all right—every three to four hours. But it's not going to be a burger, fries, and a soda.

FEEDING THE MACHINE

You need six classes of nutrients to build and drive your human body: carbohydrates, proteins, fats, vitamins, minerals, and water. The first three—carbohydrates, proteins, and fats—are what we call macronutrients. They provide energy and structure to the body's cells and tissues. The other nutrients regulate body functions and the machinery inside our cells.

Water is the most critical element in the diet. Most of the other nutrients essential for life can function only in the presence of water. Under optimal conditions, the body can survive 60 days without food but only 10 days without water. During moderate activity levels under average environmental conditions, the body needs a gallon (or nearly four liters) of water per day. Your muscles are made up of 60 to 70 percent water.

Calories are a measure of the energy value of food; they are the amount of energy you put into your body's fuel tank. If you consume more calories than you use during the course of each day, the excess energy is stored inside your body. In time, you'll gain weight. On the other hand, if you consume fewer calories than you need, you'll lose weight because your body burns fat stores in order to generate the extra energy requirement.

Designing your diet is easy, as long as you follow the steps of my hard muscle formula. It's important to remember that my fuel plan is not a starvation diet that involves an all-out restriction of food consumption. The aim of this nutritional program is to provide nutrients to build muscle and encourage fat loss. You know that quick fix starvation thing? Don't do it—it doesn't work.

The subtle changes we're going to make to your eating habits will melt away fat. Your nutrition program should be planned with intent; do not expect it to fall into place by accident. Although the process of designing your diet might seem tricky at first, it's not complicated. Once you get the hang of it, the process becomes simple. You can begin formulating your nutrition intake using the following steps. You may want a pen and paper to make your own calculations.

Step 1: Caloric Balance

The first step is to calculate your daily calorie requirement (DCR). This figure represents the amount of calories you need to perform daily activities. It's what

I call the "maintenance calorie requirement"—the number of calories needed per day to maintain your current body weight. This simple calculation is made using the following formula:

Body weight in pounds × 10 = DCR

Let's say you weigh 180 pounds (81.6 kg). Your daily maintenance calorie requirement is 180 × 10, or 1,800 calories. Consume more than this amount per day, and you'll gain weight because your body is in a positive caloric balance. Eat fewer calories than this amount, and you'll lose weight because your body is in a negative caloric balance.

This calculation is a rough estimate of daily calorie intake. Remember that the amount of calories you use varies from day to day depending on the level of activity. If your goal is to lose body fat, your daily calorie intake should be 10 percent less than your maintenance requirement so that you're in a negative caloric balance. If, on the other hand, your goal is to gain weight, your daily calorie intake should be 10 percent more that the maintenance value to ensure that you're in a positive caloric balance.

Step 2: Timing

The timing and spacing of your daily meals are important. You need to consider the number of meals consumed per day and the size of each meal. I recommend that you eat five or six small meals every three to four hours during the day rather than stuffing yourself with the traditional triple feasts at breakfast, lunch, and dinner.

There are several reasons for this strategy. First, eating every few hours maintains a constant energy level. You won't feel lethargic between meals. Second, if you have extended gaps between meals, you become so hungry that you're tempted to overeat at the next sitting. The excess calories are likely stored as fat. Third, when you consume smaller meals, your stomach adapts by reducing in size. A smaller stomach requires less food to fill it, and you'll prevent that bloated belly look. Finally, the amount of food your intestine can digest and absorb in one sitting is limited. For example, your gut is capable of extracting only 30 to 40 grams of protein from a single meal of solid food. If you consume larger meals, any excess nutrients may pass through without being absorbed, going to waste.

If you sleep 6 to 8 hours each night, that means you're awake for 16 to 18 hours during each 24-hour period. Fitting six meals into your day means eating every 2 to 3 hours. To calculate how many calories you need to consume at each meal to make up your daily calorie requirement, divide your DCR by 6. Go back to our example of the 180-pound person who requires 1,800 calories per day. When his DCR is divided by 6, it breaks down to 300 calories per meal. You see what I mean when I say you won't go hungry on this diet?

When planning your six daily meals, list them as meals one through six, or, if you prefer tradition, call the meals breakfast, lunch, dinner, and supper, interspersed with nutritious midmorning and midafternoon snacks. You're allowed to juggle the calorie content of each meal as long as the total amount over the course of the day meets your daily calorie requirement. The diet plan for a 180-pound person doesn't have to be six 300-calorie meals. A person of that body weight might choose the following meal plan:

▶ Breakfast: 300 calories

▶ Midmorning snack: 150 calories

▶ Lunch: 500 calories

▶ Midafternoon snack: 150 calories

▶ Dinner: 500 calories

▶ Evening snack: 200 calories

Just make sure that your daily total—in this case, 1,800 calories—matches your daily requirement.

Step 3: Nutrients

The third step of the hard muscle formula is to adjust the relative proportion of nutrients that make up your daily intake of fuel. Coordinating the nutrient ratios in your diet is called food partitioning. I recommend a diet that is low in fat and high in protein. The relative proportion of each nutrient in your diet is shown in table 6.1.

The three dietary macronutrients that provide energy for your body are carbohydrates, protein, and fat. Not all nutrients are made equal, so the relative proportion of each is an important determinant of your overall calorie intake. Water and the dietary micronutrients (vitamins and minerals) do not directly contribute to your daily calorie intake, but they are essential components of a healthy diet.

TABLE 6.1

Macronutrient Ratios for Weight Gain and Weight Loss

	Weight gain	Weight loss
Protein	40%	50%
Carbohydrates	50%	40%
Fat	10%	10%
Calorie balance	Positive	Negative

Dietary fat (nine calories per gram) has more than twice the amount of calories per gram than protein or carbohydrates (four calories per gram). Why is this important? Well, let's say you want to consume 100 calories. You could provide this amount by eating 11 grams of fat, but if you choose a protein or carbohydrate source, you'd get to eat 25 grams, twice the amount of food.

Dietary fat is relatively high in calories, so a diet that contains a lot of fat will amount to a large number of calories. A low-fat diet contains fewer calories, allowing you to eat more substance. In other words, for 100 calories you could eat a good-sized portion of tuna (protein) or rice (carbohydrates), but only a tiny chunk of cheese (fat). Your hunger will be better satisfied if your stomach is filled with tuna or rice rather than merely teased by a mouse-sized portion of cheese, right?

Protein

Proteins are large nitrogen-rich molecules made up of a long string of amino acids. Protein is a fundamental component of all living cells and is essential for the growth and repair of tissue. The term protein is derived from the Greek *proteios,* which means first. Protein provides the amino acid building blocks for muscle, and its high nitrogen content creates the right anabolic environment for muscle growth. When it comes to building muscle and losing body fat, protein is the king of all nutrients.

To build muscle, you need an adequate supply of raw materials. Sufficient protein is essential for building lean muscle mass. To get your fill, aim to consume between 1.0 to 1.5 grams of protein per body weight. A person who weighs 180 pounds should try to eat at least 180 grams of protein each day. The DCR of a person weighing 180 pounds is 1,800 calories, so if protein is to make up 50 percent of the DCR, he will need to consume the protein equivalent of 900 calories. To meet this daily requirement, every meal should contain at least 30 grams of protein.

Protein is the key to building muscle and trimming fat.

Daily protein intake = 1 to 1.5 grams per pound of body weight

A high-protein diet is less likely to cause fat deposits than either a high-carb or high-fat diet. There are several reasons for this. First, many of the calories from protein are burned off during digestion through what is called the thermic effect of food. Of all the macronutrients, protein has the highest thermic effect; digestion burns off 25 percent of the calories consumed. In comparison, only 15 percent of the calories from carbs are used during digestion. Fat has virtually no thermic effect.

Second, unlike carbs, protein does not stimulate a significant insulin response. Insulin, a storage hormone, neutralizes blood sugar and is responsible for depositing fat. Because the effect of protein on insulin secretion is negligible, the potential for fat storage is diminished.

Third, protein consumption stimulates the secretion of glucagon, a hormone that opposes the effect of insulin. Since glucagon is a signal to burn fat for fuel, fat loss rather than fat gain tends to occur.

So, the larger the protein component of your diet, the more effective are your powers of fat burning. There's no evidence that a high-protein diet has any

TABLE 6.2

Biological Values of Protein Sources

Protein source	Biological value (BV)
Whey protein	100+
Milk	100
Egg whites	88
Fish	83
Beef	80
Chicken	79
Soy	74

TABLE 6.3

Sources of 30 Grams of Protein

30 grams of protein equal
1 chicken breast (6 oz)
1 turkey breast (6 oz)
6 oz tuna
6 oz fish
6 oz lean beef
5 egg whites (large)
30 fluid oz nonfat milk

detrimental effect on healthy people with normal kidney function, but it's recommended that a high-protein diet be accompanied by drinking lots of fluids. Adequate liquid consumption—at least a gallon of water a day—helps flush your body of any protein by-products.

Quality sources of dietary protein include beef, poultry, fish, egg whites, and milk. However, not all protein sources are created equal; some are better for building muscle than others. In fact, every protein source has a biological value (BV) that determines the quality of its protein content. The higher the BV, the better the protein is absorbed and used for muscle growth. So when it comes to choosing a protein source, pick the ones with the highest BV. The BV of different protein sources is compared in table 6.2.

Selecting a portion of protein to accompany each meal is not difficult. Each portion should contain about 30 grams of protein. The easiest way to check is to read the product label for a breakdown of its contents. For easy reference, use table 6.3 as a guide.

Carbohydrates

Carbohydrates are sugar molecules and your body's preferred source of energy. Dietary carbohydrates are found in foods such as sugars, starches, and fiber. Carbohydrates come in two forms: simple and complex.

Simple sugars (monosaccharides and disaccharides) such as glucose, fructose, and sucrose are found in cane sugar and fruits. Simple sugars are quick-fix sources of energy. They have a high glycemic index (GI), which means they are absorbed quickly by the gut, causing a rapid increase in blood sugar.

Complex carbohydrates are larger polysaccharide molecules that provide a more sustained release of energy (lower GI). Complex carbohydrates include starches (potatoes, pasta, and rice) and fiber (vegetables, cereals, and whole grains). Dietary carbohydrates with a lower GI are digested and absorbed slowly, maintaining a stable concentration of sugar in the blood.

The body converts carbohydrates into glucose for energy or into glycogen for energy storage in the liver and muscle. When glycogen stores are filled, excess carbohydrates are converted to fat. Even though dietary carbs are essential for energy and muscle building, eating more carbohydrates than you need feeds your fat stores, inflating that spare tire around your waist.

Quality sources of complex carbohydrates include rice, potatoes, pasta, yams, oatmeal, and whole-wheat bread. Whole foods such as potatoes, yams, and fruits are carbohydrates that nature has portioned out for us. One medium-sized potato is a single portion of carbohydrates to complement one of your daily meals. Table 6.4 itemizes single 25- to 30-gram portions of carbohydrates from a selection of dietary sources.

Remember that to partition your nutrient ratio of 50 percent protein to 40 percent carbohydrates (for weight loss), the portion of carbohydrates in each meal should be slightly less than that of protein. If you're shooting for 30 to 35 grams of protein per meal, the amount of carbohydrates should be about 25 to 30 grams.

TABLE 6.4

Sources of 25 Grams of Carbohydrates

25 grams of carbohydrates equal*
30 g rice
30 g pasta
40 g oatmeal
1 medium potato
1 piece of fruit
8 fluid oz fruit juice

* Approximate values

FRUIT

Fruits are high in vitamins, minerals, and fiber. That's the good news. The bad news is fruit contains the simple sugar fructose. Fructose produces a stable rise in blood sugar, but it has a downside for anyone trying to lose fat.

One problem is that fructose is readily converted into body fat. This means a proportion of the fruit you eat can ultimately end up as fat. What's more, high-fructose corn syrup is the main sweetener in soda. The regular consumption of soda has been linked to the rise in obesity rates. A second problem is that fructose can cause your body to absorb extra fat from meals. Drinking juice or a soda with a meal encourages fat uptake. Third, fructose does not efficiently restock the muscle's energy store of glycogen, which means you might not recover from your workouts effectively. After exercise, starchy and fibrous carbohydrates, such as potatoes and rice, restock more glycogen into the muscles than simple sugars do, which promotes recovery. With just a fraction of simple sugars being converted to glycogen, the remaining likely spill into fat stores.

To achieve that lean, muscular look, select complex carbohydrates instead of fruit. If you choose to get your daily dose of vitamins and minerals from fruit, that's okay, but remember—everything in moderation. By all means, choose your favorite piece of fruit. Bananas, oranges, apples, grapefruits, melons, peaches, strawberries, and blueberries are all very nutritious, but a single daily serving is all you need. Too much whole fruit or juice forms fat on the body.

If you're aiming for that extremely ripped look by reducing your body fat below 10 percent, you might notice a significant difference in your physique when you eliminate fruits and juices from your diet. Many competitive bodybuilders looking to get shredded don't include fruit in their precontest diets. If you choose to totally eliminate fruit from your diet for a short period of time, be sure to take a daily multivitamin and mineral supplement to prevent deficiency.

FIBER

Fiber, plant material resistant to digestion, is essential for proper digestion and prevents constipation. Dietary sources of fiber include bran, cereals, whole grains, vegetables, oatmeal, fruit, and brown rice. To keep your digestive tract running smoothly, the recommended daily intake of fiber is 25 grams.

VEGETABLES

Vegetables are healthy low-calorie foods. They are not a major source of carbohydrates or protein, but you should include a vegetable with two of your daily meals. Their primary benefits are that they are high in fiber and contain vitamins and antioxidants. They do you good! Quality sources include broccoli, carrots, spinach, lettuce, tomatoes, cucumbers, green beans, squash, cabbage, and mushrooms. Buy your veggies fresh or frozen, not canned. Frozen veggies are convenient and just as nutritious as fresh. Serve them lightly steamed or raw.

Dietary Fat

Fats are molecules containing strings of fatty acids. In addition to being the body's alternative energy source to glucose, fats have several important functions.

▶ Fat is an essential component of cell structure and nerves.

▶ The insulating layer of fat beneath the skin helps preserve body heat.

▶ Steroid hormones, including testosterone, are made from cholesterol.

▶ Fat is required to transport fat-soluble vitamins through the body.

Now don't forget that your body has plenty of stored fat already. What's more, your body is able to synthesize most of the fat it needs, with the exception of the so-called essential fats such as the omega-3 and omega-6 fatty acids. Small amounts of these unsaturated fats are essential in the diet because your body can't make them. So not all dietary fat is bad. Saturated fats, found in butter, animal fat, egg yolks, and lard, are the enemy. As a rule, you can identify bad fat because it's solid at room temperature. The healthier monounsaturated and polyunsaturated fats are liquid at room temperature. Examples of unsaturated fat sources include olive oil, flaxseed oil, canola oil, fish oil, sesame oil, safflower oil, and nuts.

Too much fat is unhealthy, period. It leads to obesity, diabetes, and an increased risk of heart disease. Excess dietary fat raises LDL (bad) cholesterol and lowers HDL (good) cholesterol. The result is clogged arteries, high blood pressure, and heart attacks. You can avoid all this by sticking to a low-fat diet. You certainly shouldn't be concerned with *adding* fat to your diet. Even with the best efforts to eliminate fat, the stuff finds its way into your diet. As you can see in table 6.5, small amounts of fat are in many of the foods we eat.

The recommended daily intake of fat is 20 percent of your total calories. But if you want to ditch that spare tire, aim to

TABLE 6.5

Dietary Fat Sources

Food source	Fat (grams)
Skinless chicken breast (6 oz)	6
6 oz water-packed tuna	2
Lean beef (6 oz)	10
1 whole egg	4
Oatmeal (40 g / 1.25 oz)	3

keep your fat intake around 10 percent, which amounts to 15 to 20 grams a day. Even when you try diligently to restrict your fat intake, at the end of the day, it'll probably creep up toward 20 percent without your realizing it. If you want to add some healthy polyunsaturated fat to your diet, use a tablespoon of flaxseed or canola oil mixed with vinegar as a salad dressing. Alternatively, a few servings of fish each week provide adequate amounts of good fat.

Vitamins and Minerals

Vitamins and minerals are essential dietary micronutrients. They serve many functions in the body, and dietary deficiency can result in ill health. Although these micronutrients don't themselves enhance athletic performance, they're necessary to achieve optimal levels of performance.

A well-balanced diet provides all the essential vitamins and minerals. But if you're involved in an intense exercise program, you'll require additional amounts of certain micronutrients. The simple solution to avoid deficiency is to take a daily multivitamin and mineral supplement. You have enough dietary concerns without worrying about individual vitamin or mineral consumption. If you pay too much attention to these micronutrients, you might miss the bigger picture. Nevertheless, a few micronutrients, such as vitamins B, C, and E and calcium, deserve a brief discussion for those participating in regular exercise.

The B-complex family of vitamins is important for metabolism and energy production. Vitamin C has an important role in postexercise recovery in that it's needed for the synthesis of collagen and the repair of tissues, such as muscle and tendons. Vitamin C might also minimize delayed-onset muscle soreness following exercise. Because many athletes have suboptimal levels of vitamin C, supplementing the diet with 500 to 1,000 milligrams per day might enhance overall performance. Both vitamins C and E are powerful antioxidants. Vitamin E protects against harmful free radicals generated during exercise and thereby boosts immunity. Beneficial effects are obtained with daily doses of 400 IUs. Calcium is essential for strong bones; the recommended daily intake is 1,000 to 1,200 milligrams.

Water

Last but not least on the list of essential nutrients is water. Your body is 60 to 70 percent water, and good old H_2O is essential to life. Remember to consume at least a gallon (nearly 4 liters) of water a day. Unlike most other thirst quenchers, water is calorie free.

PLANNING MEALS

Selecting the content of your diet is easy. You can create six healthy meals each day by using the food chart in table 6.6. Choose a portion of protein and

TABLE 6.6

Food Choices

	Food sources
Protein	Skinless chicken breast
	Turkey breast, lean ground turkey
	Salmon, water-packed tuna
	Lean ground beef, top sirloin steak, top round steak
	Egg whites
	Lean ham
	Low-fat cottage cheese
Carbohydrates	Rice, pasta
	Potato, yam
	Oatmeal, whole-wheat bread
	Orange, apple, banana, melon, grapefruit

carbohydrates from each section to make a meal. Add a serving of vegetables to at least two of your daily meals. Healthy vegetable choices include carrots, broccoli, spinach, green beans, peas, lettuce, tomato, cucumber, green pepper, and celery.

You need to eat clean to be lean. If your diet consists of "clean" food, you reduce the chance of consuming hidden calories that appear during food preparation or as flavoring. Try to avoid using cooking fats or oils. Eat sauces, marinades, and food dressings sparingly. These seemingly innocent additions can significantly bump up the calorie count of your meal by adding extra fat and carbohydrates. For instance, a single serving of sauce, margarine spread, or marinade contains 40 calories or more. If you need to add some flavor, try spices or mustard or a tablespoon of ketchup, which contains only 15 calories of carbohydrate.

I'll remind you again here to think before you drink. A glass of most beverages, including soda, juice, beer, or wine, contains 100 calories or more. When possible, drink water.

As you gain experience in creating nutritious meals, you can make a calorie count to compare to your daily requirement calculation. Reading product labels is the best way to go. If the food is clean, it's easier to approximate your calorie intake. Use a calculator to figure how your daily intake of nutrients matches up to the protein-carb-fat split of 50-40-10. Adjust your eating as necessary.

PREPARATION

Preparing your meals is straightforward, but following a few simple rules can't hurt. You may also want to abandon or take a critical look at some of your old cooking habits. The key principle in preparation is to avoid adding additional calories, particularly from fat.

Solid meats, such as chicken, turkey breast, fish, and steak, can be grilled, baked, or broiled. Squeeze some lemon juice over the meat or lightly paste with a low-fat marinade. Don't forget to remove the skin from chicken and turkey (or use skinless cuts). Don't deep fry meat or smother it with butter or high-fat sauce. Lean ground beef or turkey can be heated in a nonstick pan. Drain off any fat or water accumulated during cooking. If you really want to clean the meat, put the cooked meat into a sieve, rinse it with water, and then reheat it before serving.

Egg whites can be scrambled in a nonstick pan with or without a nonfat cooking spray. Crack open the egg and remove the yolk. Each egg white contains six grams of protein, so you'll need five or six large eggs to get enough protein for a meal. Add one half or one whole yolk, if you wish. Cook eggs until dry to get rid of salmonella bacteria.

Other sources of protein, such as water-packed tuna or low-fat cottage cheese, don't require any preparation.

For carbohydrates, potatoes can be baked, boiled, or cooked in a microwave oven. Don't add butter or sour cream. Steam your rice. Boil your pasta. Check food labels to calculate a 25- to 30-gram portion of carbohydrates. Eat the pasta plain or squeeze a lemon over it. Don't use sauce, butter, or cheese. A portion of whole-wheat bread is usually two slices. Remember that if you use a low-fat spread, you'll add about 50 calories from fat.

Add a portion of vegetables to at least two of your daily meals. They are an excellent source of vitamins and dietary fiber. Serve them lightly steamed or raw; don't cook them in butter. If you require a salad dressing, mix a tablespoon of healthy unsaturated oil such as safflower with some vinegar.

Any nutrition program needs planning. If you don't have the appropriate foods available when and where you need them, you'll have a tough time sticking to your diet. If your kitchen is not stocked with the right food, you'll end up eating the wrong food. Planning your meals starts with making a detailed list before you visit the grocery store. Another tip: Don't go to the grocery store hungry. A hungry mind is less disciplined. Stick to the items on your list. Stock up on quality. If it's not on your list of healthy foods, don't buy it. Don't even look at it. When your house is free of junk food, you won't succumb to a damaging snack attack. When it comes to avoiding junk food, "out of sight, out of mind" is the best policy.

ENJOY A CHEAT DAY

Sticking to your diet requires discipline. With all that choice out there, restricting your intake can lead to cravings, and these cravings can drive you crazy. With this in mind, I'm granting you permission to cut yourself some slack. I recommend that you take one cheat day per week. On your cheat day, you can eat whatever you want. Be that kid in a candy store. Get those cravings out of your system.

Your cheat day can be any day of the week. You might choose Sunday or a day that coincides with a particular social occasion, such as a dinner party, birthday, or other gathering. Whatever day you pick, make the most of it. It won't hurt to pig out one day a week—it's the long-term dietary discipline that counts.

Dining out at cafes or restaurants is best done on your free day because you have little if any control of the calorie content of meals prepared by other people. Your cheat day also allows you to balance your diet by including nutrients you would otherwise restrict, such as healthy fats and fruit juices.

MODIFICATION

The hard muscle formula outlined in this chapter should serve as a blueprint. The calculations are a guide; nothing is carved in stone. We all metabolize foods in different ways. Just as each of us has a different body type, individual results from any nutrition program will vary. To accommodate individual variation, the blueprint might need to be modified. Your own food portions will depend on your daily calorie allowance, which in turn depends on your body weight and your daily calorie expenditure. The quantity of food in each of your daily meals will also depend on your goal—do you want to gain weight or lose weight?

If you're a lean ectomorph who wants to gain weight, you should consume additional calories in the form of carbohydrates. In such a case, the nutrient ratio should approximate that recommended in the mass generator program—50 percent carbohydrates, 40 percent protein, and 10 percent fat. On the other hand, if you're an endomorph who needs to cut back on carbohydrates to lose weight, you should follow the body fat blitz program: 50 percent protein, 40 percent carbohydrates, and 10 percent fat. To coordinate your own requirements, chart your progress each month, then adjust your daily calorie intake and carbohydrate consumption as necessary.

Remember that it's overconsuming calories that causes weight gain. No matter what you eat, if it has calories and you consume too much of it, you'll end up getting fat.

chapter 7

BODY FAT BLITZ PROGRAM

In the last two chapters we have focused on fat loss. We looked at the calorie-crunching powers of exercise and established the importance of the calorie-count and nutrient-profile in your diet. Now it's time to put these fat-burning theories into practice.

If you're looking to lose unwanted body fat quickly, this is the plan for you. I have combined a selection of resistance and aerobic exercises into a four-day workout routine that increases your metabolic rate and melts away your fat stores. To maximize calorie use, you'll perform between 10 and 15 repetitions of each weight-training exercise, keeping the rest interval between sets under 60 seconds. The fat-loss diet aims to create a daily calorie deficit so that the negative caloric balance forces your body to burn fat stores to provide energy.

PROGRAM OVERVIEW

Workout Plan

The body fat blitz program is designed to lose body fat. To promote calorie burning, the weights program emphasizes higher reps with lower resistance. Perform three sets of each exercise, using weights equal to 60 to 70 percent of your one-rep maximum. After an initial warm-up set of 15 reps, increase the weight on your second set so that your muscles fatigue with 12 reps. Then, on the final set, add more weight, and squeeze out 10 reps to failure. To keep your heart rate elevated—and to burn more calories—keep your rest intervals short. Move through the workouts at a fast pace, taking only 30 to 60 seconds of rest between sets and exercises. Aim to complete each workout within 30 to 40 minutes.

Even though you're lifting lighter weights (60 to 70 percent of your one-rep max) with a higher repetition range, training to failure on the last set of 10 reps *will* stimulate muscle hypertrophy. And remember that for every pound of lean muscle you add to your body, you'll burn an extra 30 calories per day at rest. So training to failure, especially on the final "work" set, is your goal for each exercise. The more muscle you possess, the more calories you burn during a workout.

The body fat blitz routine uses an upper body–lower body two-way, split-weight training system combined with two cardio workouts. I'll explain how the schedule works. Session 1 works the entire upper body (chest, shoulders, back, arms). Session 2 consists of aerobic exercise and an abdominal workout. Session 3 works the lower body (quads, hamstrings, calves). Session 4 is another combined aerobic and abdominal workout.

The prime objective of this program is *lean* muscle mass. You're striving to burn calories and shed unwanted body fat. The two sessions per week of weight training will also build muscle. And by increasing your fat-free mass (muscle), you become more efficient at burning calories. Whether you burn 300 calories by lifting weights or cycling on a stationary bike, 300 calories is 300 calories. Although aerobics don't increase muscle mass, your body recovers quickly after cardio, so you can use this form of calorie-burning exercise (every day if necessary) without worrying about overtraining.

During the weight-training sessions, you'll burn more calories by using unilateral (single-limb) training on selected exercises. By training one side at a time, you can rest one limb while the other works, so you won't need as much rest between sets. Each limb gets adequate rest, but your cardiovascular system gets less rest. Because you're training one side at a time, your workouts will take a little longer, but you'll be doing more work with less total rest and thus burning more calories. Examples of unilateral exercises included in this program are dumbbell curls, leg extensions, and leg curls.

Calorie-burning cardiovascular exercise is a key part of any fat-loss program. This continuous low-resistance exercise must be performed for at least 20 to 30 minutes to achieve an adequate training effect. Work hard enough to maintain your heart rate in the target zone—70 percent of your maximum heart rate. (Calculate your target heart rate by subtracting your age from 220, then multiplying this figure by 0.7.)

The type of aerobic exercise you do is up to you. There are many indoor and outdoor activities to choose from, including walking, jogging, cycling, stair climbing, jumping rope, and swimming. It's more challenging if you vary the aerobic exercise, selecting a different activity for each cardio session. For example, cycle on a stationary bike during session 2, then walk or jog on the treadmill during session 4. Once you have completed 30 minutes of cardio, you'll do 10 minutes of abdominal exercises to round off the session. The exercises included in this program target all areas of your midsection—the upper and lower portions of your abs, the obliques, and the serratus muscles. Remember that any abdominal work will only be *visibly* evident if your body fat percentage is 10 percent or less.

Nutrition Plan

To lose body fat, burn more calories than you consume. Being in a negative caloric balance forces the body to burn fat stores to generate extra energy. Just how many calories should you consume each day during your fat-loss program? First, calculate your maintenance daily calorie requirement (body weight in pounds multiplied by 10). Then subtract 10 percent from this amount to get your daily calorie intake for fat-burning purposes. In other words, you are depriving your body of 10 percent fewer calories than it needs for energy production on a daily basis. To meet this energy deficit, your body gets the extra calories by burning body fat.

Next, decide which food sources your calories will come from. To promote fat loss, you'll need to cut back on the ratio of carbohydrates in your diet. Divide the nutrients as follows: 50 percent protein, 40 percent carbohydrates, and 10 percent fat.

The 1,600-calorie sample meal plan (table 7.1) is a rough guide for someone who weighs 180 pounds (81.6 kg). The daily calorie intake is equivalent to an 1,800-calorie maintenance value minus 10 percent, which brings the calorie total to 1,620 calories. The daily calorie intake for losing fat is determined by calculating your maintenance calorie requirement (body weight in pounds multiplied by 10), then subtracting 10 percent from this value. So if your body weight is 180 pounds, your maintenance requirement is 180 × 10, or 1,800 calories per day. Since 10 percent of this figure is 180 calories, your daily intake should be 1,800 – 180, or 1,620 calories.

Adjusting the sample meal plan to your weight is easy. As you might recall from chapter 4, one gram of protein is four calories, one gram of carbohydrates is four calories, and one gram of fat is nine calories. Every 10 pounds (4.5 kg) in

TABLE 7.1

Body Fat Blitz Sample Meal Plan

Breakfast	Egg white scramble: Mix five egg whites with one tbsp of nonfat milk. Cook in a nonstick pan coated with a nonfat cooking spray. Serve on one piece of whole-wheat toast. Drink one cup of black coffee or water. Calories: 230
Midmorning snack	Meal-replacement drink: Mix one sachet of a meal-replacement powder such as MESO-Tech (MuscleTech) with 12 oz of cold water in a blender. Calories: 340
Lunch	Tuna meal: Drain one 6 oz can of water-packed tuna and squeeze some lemon juice over it. Serve with one portion (50 g) of steamed rice. Drink a glass of ice water. Calories: 300
Midafternoon snack	Protein drink: Mix one serving of protein powder such as NITRO-Tech (MuscleTech) with 4 oz water and 4 oz nonfat milk. Add one whole banana. Blend at high speed for 30 seconds. Calories: 240
Dinner	Chicken meal: Prepare a skinless chicken breast by squeezing lemon juice over it. Grill until cooked. Serve with a 50 g portion of steamed brown rice and spinach or broccoli. 1 tbsp of tomato ketchup is optional. Calories: 380
Late-evening snack	Eat half a low-carb protein bar such as NITRO-Tech bar (MuscleTech). Calories: 150
Daily values (approximate)	Protein: 200 g (800 cal), 50% Carbs: 160 g (640 cal), 40% Fat: 17 g (160 cal), 10% Total calories: 1,600

body weight is equivalent to 100 calories. Keeping the nutrient ratio at 50 percent protein and 40 percent carbohydrates, 100 calories equals 15 grams of protein (60 calories) plus 10 grams of carbohydrates (40 calories). To increase or decrease the calorie content to match your body weight, add or subtract these amounts from the sample meal plan.

Adjust your protein intake by changing the amount of protein powder added to your midafternoon snack or by changing the number of egg whites at breakfast (one egg white contains six grams of protein). Similarly, by adjusting the portions of pasta or rice at lunch and dinner, you can increase or decrease your intake of carbohydrates. But remember that the nutrition values in the sample meal plan are only approximate. I strongly recommend that you check nutrition labels on the products you eat because values vary among brands. Supplementing your diet with a fat-burner (see chapter 10) will also help promote fat loss.

Adjust the content of the sample meal plan to match your individual body weight, using table 7.2.

TABLE 7.2

Daily Calorie Intake Based on Body Weight (Body Fat Blitz)

Body weight (lbs)	Calories per day	Protein	Carbohydrates	Fat
220	2,000	250 g/1,000 cal	200 g/800 cal	22 g/200 cal
200	1,800	225 g/900 cal	180 g/720 cal	20 g/180 cal
180	1,600	200 g/800 cal	160 g/640 cal	18 g/160 cal
160	1,400	175 g/700 cal	140 g/560 cal	16 g/140 cal
140	1,200	150 g/600 cal	120 g/480 cal	14 g/120 cal

Nutrient ratio: 50% protein, 40% carbohydrates, 10% fat

Calorie value: 1 g protein = 4 calories; 1 g carbohydrates = 4 calories; 1 g fat = 9 calories

Daily calorie intake = (body weight in pounds × 10) – 10%

Progress Measurements

You'll be recording data in two categories: shape and function. In the shape category, record body weight using a scale; measure waist circumference with a tape measure. You can also measure your body fat percentage using a skin caliper. Follow the manufacturer's instructions and record the skin thickness at three sites on your body (typically, the upper arm, waist, and thigh). Calculate the average reading by adding all three measurements, then dividing by three. The average body fat percentage for males is about 15 percent, but a sleek six-pack of abs will only show if your body fat is below 10 percent.

In the function category, evaluate your fitness during an aerobic exercise of your choice, such as cycling or jogging. Monitor how long you can sustain your heart rate at 70 percent of the maximum. Calculate your target heart rate by subtracting your age from 220 and then multiplying by 0.7. A person of average fitness should be able to sustain 70 percent of maximum heart rate for 20 minutes. Each week, aim to increase your cardio time by 10 minutes or increase your target heart rate by 5 percent. The harder you work for 30 minutes, the more calories you'll burn. The more calories burned, the greater the fat loss. You can also measure muscle strength by recording the maximum weight you can lift during the last set of each exercise. The stronger the muscle becomes, the bigger it grows. The larger your muscle mass, the more fat you'll burn. Aim to increase the weight on each exercise by 5 percent every two weeks.

Results

After six weeks on this program, you should lose four to six pounds of body fat—about a pound a week. During this time you'll slice an inch off your waist circumference and record a 5 percent drop in body fat.

BODY FAT BLITZ WORKOUT

Body Fat Blitz Exercise Program

Routine: Upper–lower two-way split
Cycle: Four days per week
Schedule: Monday, Tuesday, Thursday, Friday
Goal: Lose body fat
Detail: 3 sets of 15, 12, 10 reps
Rest interval: 30 to 60 seconds
Workout time: 40 minutes

UPPER BODY MONDAY	
Chest	Cable crossovers Incline dumbbell presses
Shoulders	Seated dumbbell lateral raises Dumbbell shoulder presses
Back	Wide-grip pulldowns Seated cable rows
Arms	Dumbbell curls Triceps pushdowns
CARDIO AND ABS TUESDAY	
Cardio	Cycling (30 minutes)
Abs	Twisting sit-ups Vertical leg raises

LOWER BODY THURSDAY	
Quadriceps	Unilateral leg extensions Machine squats
Hamstrings	Unilateral leg curls
Calves	Donkey calf raises
CARDIO AND ABS FRIDAY	
Cardio	Treadmill (30 minutes) walking or jogging.
Abs	Floor crunches Dumbbell pullovers

UPPER BODY (MONDAY)
Chest

CABLE CROSSOVERS

This is a great isolation exercise for the middle and lower portions of the chest muscle. The maneuver should resemble a bear hug. Stand in the center of the cable crossover machine. With palms turned down, grasp the D-shaped handles attached to the cables coming from the high pulleys (figure 7.1a). Place your feet firmly on the ground about shoulder-width apart. From this crucifix-like position, squeeze the handles down simultaneously in front of your body until your hands meet at hip level (figure 7.1b). Hold the contracted position for one second, tightening your chest muscles. Your torso should be tilted forward slightly at the waist. Keep your elbows bent slightly throughout the movement. Slowly return to the start position. Keep your palms turned down and feel your chest muscles stretch. Hold at the start position for a second and then repeat.

> ▶ **CHECK IT!** Tilt your torso forward about 25 degrees in relation to the floor. Keep elbows slightly bent with palms turned down. Don't allow your hands to travel above shoulder level; this releases tension from your chest muscles and places your shoulder joint in a vulnerable position.

Figure 7.1 Cable crossovers: *(a)* grab the cable handles; *(b)* bring hands in front of your body.

Chest *(continued)*

INCLINE DUMBBELL PRESSES

Position an adjustable incline bench at a 30- to 45-degree angle. Sit on the bench, grab a dumbbell in each hand, and rest one on each thigh. As you lean back onto the bench, position the dumbbells alongside your chest, palms turned forward (figure 7.2a). Position your feet firmly on the floor for stability. From the start position, press the weights vertically upward over your upper chest (figure 7.2b). Bring the dumbbells together as you raise them. Squeeze your upper chest muscles for one second in the top position, elbows straight. Bending your elbows, lower the weights slowly back to the start position. Hold the dumbbells level with your chest momentarily and repeat. Inhale on the way down; exhale as you push up. The path the dumbbells travel should be perpendicular to the floor, not to your body.

> ▶ **CHECK IT!** Don't set the bench at a steep angle, or you'll work your shoulders more than your upper chest.

You can also do the incline bench press using a barbell or a machine. A dumbbell chest press can be performed flat or at an inclined or declined bench angle.

Figure 7.2 Incline dumbbell presses: *(a)* get into position on an incline bench; *(b)* press the weights over your chest.

Shoulders

SEATED DUMBBELL LATERAL RAISES

Sit upright on the edge of a flat exercise bench. Hold a dumbbell in each hand at arms' length, hanging down by your sides with palms turned in (figure 7.3a). Raise the dumbbells up and out to the sides until they're level with your chin (figure 7.3b). Keep your palms turned down during the lift. Your arms should be slightly bent but elbows kept stiff during the movement. When your elbows reach shoulder level, hold the position momentarily, then lower the weight in a slow controlled fashion back to the starting position. Keep your torso upright during the movement. A slight forward tilt is okay, but don't lean backward.

> ▶ **CHECK IT!** Don't raise the dumbbells too high because this places undue stress on the shoulders. Your hands should be level with your chin, with elbows just below shoulder height. There should be no movement of the elbows.

You can also do this exercise with one arm at a time. Grab the side of the bench with your free hand to stabilize your torso.

Figure 7.3 Seated dumbbell lateral raises: *(a)* hold dumbbells at your sides; *(b)* raise the weights.

85

Shoulders *(continued)*

DUMBBELL SHOULDER PRESSES

Sit on a bench with the backrest upright at a vertical angle. If the backrest is adjustable, tilt it back 15 to 20 degrees to optimize body position. Hold a dumbbell in each hand, palms turned forward, and lift to shoulder level. Your elbows should point out to the sides. Firmly position your feet on the floor and lean back onto the bench (figure 7.4a). Press the dumbbells up until your elbows are extended fully overhead (figure 7.4b). Pause momentarily, contracting your deltoid muscles. Slowly lower the weights to shoulder level. Pause for one second and then repeat.

> ▶ **CHECK IT!** Don't allow the dumbbells to stray back and forth during the movement. The weights should move in one plane, vertically up and down, perpendicular to the floor.

You can also do this exercise on a seated front press machine.

Figure 7.4 Dumbbell shoulder presses: *(a)* lean back on the bench; *(b)* press the dumbbells overhead.

Back

WIDE-GRIP PULLDOWNS

Sit at a cable pulldown machine, facing inward, and position your thighs under the pads. Grasp the bar in an overhand grip, palms turned forward, with hands about six inches wider than shoulder-width. From the start position, with arms fully extended overhead, lean your torso back about 30 degrees from the vertical plane (figure 7.5a). Begin the repetition by pulling the bar down to the top of your chest (figure 7.5b). Think of your hands as hooks. Make your upper back muscles do the work, pulling your elbows down and back. Hold the bar above your collar bone for one second, contracting the latissimus muscles. Slowly return to the start position. This exercise develops width in your back muscles.

You can also do pulldowns using a reverse, underhand grip on the bar with palms turned toward you, as described in chapter 11. If you don't have access to a pulldown machine, the same movement can be done using a chin-up bar (chapter 4).

▶ **CHECK IT!** Don't pull the bar down below the collar bone. Don't lean back too far or pull the weight down with momentum.

Figure 7.5 Wide-grip pulldowns: *(a)* arms extended overhead; *(b)* bring the bar to your chest.

Back *(continued)*

SEATED CABLE ROWS

Position yourself at a seated row station. Grab the handlebar attached to the low pulley cable with your arms extended in front of you. Place your feet shoulder-width apart on the footplate with knees locked. Sit up straight and pull your shoulders back. From the start position (figure 7.6a), pull the handlebar to your upper abdomen, moving your elbows backward as far as you can. Hold the contracted position momentarily, squeezing your back muscles (figure 7.6b). Don't lean backward. Keeping your spine straight, slowly return to the start position and repeat. This is a great exercise to build thickness and strength in the middle and lower sections of your back.

▸ **CHECK IT!** Keep your spine straight and still during this exercise. Don't lean backward or forward; don't use momentum to pull the weight.

You can perform the seated cable row using a variety of grips. The handlebar attachment affords a narrow, vertical grip with palms facing one another. Attaching a straight bar to the low cable allows you to use a wider hand spacing with an underhand or overhand grip. My personal preference is the handlebar grip.

Figure 7.6 Seated cable rows: *(a)* **hold the handlebar with arms extended;** *(b)* **pull back toward your abdomen.**

Arms

DUMBBELL CURLS

Grab a pair of dumbbells and sit on the edge of a flat bench. Start with your arms straight at your sides (figure 7.7a). Do this exercise with one arm at a time—the right arm curls first, then the left arm, and so on. With palms turned forward, bend the right elbow, lifting the dumbbell toward your right shoulder (figure 7.7b). Keep your upper arm and torso still; let your biceps do the work. When the dumbbell reaches shoulder level, pause for one second before lowering the weight slowly. When the dumbbell returns to the start position, pause momentarily while you perform the next repetition using the left arm. Alternate reps between the right and left arms until the set is complete.

Figure 7.7 Dumbbell curls: *(a)* sit on a flat bench, arms at your sides; *(b)* curl weight toward your shoulder.

Arms *(continued)*

TRICEPS PUSHDOWNS

Attach a short bar to the cable of a high pulley. Grip the bar with hands slightly closer than shoulder-width apart and palms turned down. Position upper arms perpendicular to the ground, keeping elbows in at your sides. In the start position, the bar is at nipple level and elbows bent past 90 degrees (figure 7.8a). Push the bar down toward your thighs until your arms are straight and your elbows lock (figure 7.8b). Keep upper arms close to your body. Flex your triceps at the bottom position for one count. Slowly return to the start position, hold momentarily, and repeat.

Figure 7.8 Triceps pushdowns: *(a)* grip the bar on the cable machine; *(b)* push the bar toward your thighs.

CARDIO AND ABS (TUESDAY)
Cardio

Spend 30 minutes on a stationary bike, keeping your heart rate in the target range (see page 59 for calculation).

Abs

TWISTING SIT-UPS

This exercise is a variation of the decline sit-up described on page 46. The movement incorporates a slight twist of your torso to work the serratus and oblique muscles. The decline bench should be at a 20-degree head-down angle to the floor. Position your feet under the roller pad with the backs of your knees on the knee pad. Lie back and place your hands behind your head. As you crunch up from the bottom position, direct your right elbow toward your left knee (figure 7.9). Feel the contraction in your right oblique muscles. Hold for one second, then return to the start position. During the second repetition, direct your left elbow to your right knee to work your left oblique muscles. Repeat, alternating between left and right sides.

As you gain strength, increase the number of reps or tilt the bench at a steeper angle.

▶ **CHECK IT!** Don't go back too far; this releases the tension from the abdominal muscles and places unnecessary stress on the lower back.

Figure 7.9 As you curl up, bring your elbow to the opposite knee.

Abs *(continued)*

VERTICAL LEG RAISES

Support yourself on a vertical leg raise apparatus with your elbows positioned on the pads. Grip the handles and rest your spine against the back support. Your legs should be hanging straight down, feet side by side (figure 7.10a). From the start position, raise your legs at the hips while bending your knees. Pull your thighs up toward your chest, keeping your legs together (figure 7.10b). Hold the top position momentarily, contracting your abdominals.

> ▶ **CHECK IT!** Lower your legs down slowly to keep tension on your abdominals. Don't swing your legs.

Then slowly lower your legs down to the starting position and repeat. This is a terrific exercise for your lower abdominals.

If you don't have access to a vertical leg raise apparatus, you can do this exercise hanging vertical from a chin-up bar, supporting your weight with your hands or using a pair of ab slings.

Figure 7.10 Vertical leg raises: *(a)* support your weight with your elbows; *(b)* bring your knees toward your chest.

LOWER BODY (THURSDAY)
Quadriceps

a

UNILATERAL LEG EXTENSIONS

Sit at a leg extension machine. Adjust the backrest so the back of your knee fits snugly against the seat and your whole thigh is supported. Position your ankle under the roller pad. If the pad is adjustable, position it so it rests just above your ankle on the lowest part of your shin. Grip the handles on the side of the machine for support (figure 7.11a). Using one leg at a time, contract the quadriceps to straighten one knee, while the other leg remains stationary (figure 7.11b). Lift the weight all the way up until your knee is straight. Pause for one second at the top, flexing the quadriceps muscle. Slowly lower the weight until your knee bends to 90 degrees. Hold the weight momentarily in the bottom position and repeat. Upon completion of the set number of reps,

let the fatigued leg hang down and do the exercise with the other leg.

You can also do this exercise in the standard fashion using both legs at once, as described in chapter 4. The advantage of the unilateral version is that it requires extra effort and burns more calories.

b

Figure 7.11 Unilateral leg extensions: (a) sit in the leg extension machine; (b) straighten one leg at a time.

93

Quadriceps *(continued)*

MACHINE SQUATS

Use a Smith machine if one is available. Position the bar of the machine centrally across the upper portion of your back. Stand with your feet shoulder-width apart slightly in front of the plane of your body, with toes pointing forward (figure 7.12a). This is the start position. Begin the repetition by bending your knees and slowly lowering your hips straight down until your thighs are parallel to the floor (figure 7.12b). During the movement, be sure to keep your back straight, chin up, and head looking forward. Once you reach the bottom position, push the weight up using your thighs and hips

> ▶ **CHECK IT!** To reduce the chance of knee injury, avoid squatting below parallel. Position your feet about six inches in front of the plane of your body during machine squats.

until your knees are straight. On a Smith machine, the movement occurs in a single plane vertically up and down perpendicular to the floor. Inhale deeply during the descent and exhale on the way up.

Figure 7.12 Machine squats: *(a)* **get into position in the machine;** *(b)* **lower the weight by bending your knees.**

Hamstrings

UNILATERAL LEG CURLS

Using an upright leg curl machine, position one ankle under the roller pad and support your weight with the other leg (figure 7.13a). Lean forward and grip the handles for support. From the start position, curl the weight up by bending your knee (figure 7.13b). Try to bring your heel to your buttock. When the roller pad touches the back of your hamstrings, hold the contracted position for one second. Slowly return the weight to the start position with your leg almost straight. Hold at the bottom momentarily and repeat. After you've completed the set number of reps with one leg, do the same for the opposite leg.

This exercise can be performed in an upright position using a kneeling leg curl machine as shown or a standing leg curl machine. Unilateral leg curls also can be performed on the lying leg curl machine, as described in chapter 4.

Figure 7.13 Unilateral leg curls: *(a)* kneel in the upright leg curl machine; *(b)* bring heel toward buttock.

Calves

a

DONKEY CALF RAISES

Place a calf block (or a three-inch block of wood) in front of an exercise bench. Position the balls of your feet on the block, bend forward at the hips, and support your upper body on the bench. Have your training partner sit astride your hips so that his body weight is directly above your calf muscles. Keeping your knees locked, lower your heels, stretching out your calf muscles (figure 7.14a). From the start position, raise your heels as high as you can, lifting your partner's weight vertically upward. At the top position,

▶ **CHECK IT!** Keep your back straight; keep your knees stiff but slightly bent.

b

squeeze your calf muscles and hold for a one count (figure 7.14b). Slowly lower your heels back to the start position. Hold the stretch momentarily and repeat.

You can also do the straight-leg donkey calf raise on a calf machine where the weight is transmitted through a pad that rests across your lower back. If you don't have a training partner or access to this type of calf machine, do standing calf raises, as described in chapter 4.

Figure 7.14 Donkey calf raises: (a) get into position on the calf block; (b) raise your heels upward.

CARDIO AND ABS (FRIDAY)

Cardio

Spend 30 minutes on a treadmill, keeping your heart rate within target range (see page 59 for calculation). Walk briskly or jog, depending on your level of fitness.

Abs

FLOOR CRUNCHES

Lie on the floor with your hands beside your head. Bring your knees together and place your feet flat on the floor about a foot from your buttocks (figure 7.15a). Begin the exercise by pushing your lower back into the floor. Roll your shoulders up, keeping your knees and hips still (figure 7.15b). Crunch your chest forward until your abs are fully contracted. Your shoulders will raise only a few inches off the floor. Keep your lower spine in contact with the floor. Hold the contracted position for one second, lower your shoulders, and repeat. This exercise works the upper portion of your abdominals.

You can also do this exercise on an abdominal crunch machine (page 168).

Figure 7.15 Floor crunches: *(a)* **lie on the floor with your hands beside your head;** *(b)* **raise your shoulders off the floor.**

Abs *(continued)*

DUMBBELL PULLOVERS

This is not a typical abdominal exercise, but it does develop the fingerlike serratus muscles that fan out from the armpits into the upper abs. The exercise helps expand the rib cage and feels therapeutic when you're out of breath immediately after a cardio session. Lie supine across a flat exercise bench with only your upper back resting on the bench. Position your feet firmly on the floor to stabilize your lower torso. Grab a dumbbell by placing your palms against the inside of the plates at one end, positioning your hands together so that your index fingers and thumbs form a diamond shape. Extend your arms straight up above your head so that the dumbbell hangs directly over your face (figure 7.16a). From this start position, lower the dumbbell backward until your hands pass just below the level of your head (figure 7.16b). Your arms should bend slightly during the movement. Inhale deeply as you lower the weight and achieve a full stretch on the rib cage. Pull the weight back to the start position, following the same wide arc, exhaling as you do so.

> ► **CHECK IT!** Deep breathing is essential during this exercise. Don't let your arms extend too far behind your head because this risks shoulder injury.

You can also perform this exercise using a pullover machine.

Figure 7.16 Dumbbell pullovers: *(a)* **hold the dumbbell over your face;** *(b)* **lower the dumbbell.**

FURTHER FAT LOSS

The keys to fat loss are the three Cs: cardio, calories, and carbs. If you reach a plateau or sticking point in your body fat percentage, here are three possible solutions:

1. Increase your cardio by extending the duration of aerobic exercise to 45 to 60 minutes or adding extra sessions of aerobics to your weekly schedule.

2. Reduce your calorie intake by omitting your cheat day, reducing the number of meals you eat, or subtracting 5 to 10 percent increments from your daily total calorie intake.

3. Cut back your carbs by eliminating them from your last meal of the day or gradually reducing carb portions so that the nutrient ratio of your diet moves toward 60 percent protein, 30 percent carbs, and 10 percent fat.

Remember that your energy levels fall as you deplete your intake of carbohydrates. It's tough to maintain a diet that contains only 30 percent carbohydrates (around 100 grams per day) for longer than a few weeks. Many competitive bodybuilders practice *decarbing* and *carbing up* during the week before a contest. For the first three days, carbohydrate intake is reduced to 100 grams per day. Then carbs are reintroduced at rates of 200, 300, and 400 grams per day during the lead-up to the show. The process of carbing up restocks glycogen stores in the muscles to make them look full, hard, and defined on contest day.

If you really want to drop your body fat percentage quickly, the sample low-carb diet shown in table 7.3 will burn body fat with extreme prejudice when combined with daily sessions of cardio.

TABLE 7.3

High-Protein/Low-Carb Sample Meal Plan

Meal 1	Six egg whites, scrambled Half a grapefruit Calories: 250
Meal 2	Two 6 oz cans of tuna with 40 g rice Calories: 450
Meal 3	6 oz lean beef with 40 g rice Calories: 350
Meal 4	Protein shake Calories: 250
Meal 5	One 6 oz chicken breast Calories: 200
Daily totals (approximate)	Protein: 225 g (60%) Carbs: 112 g (30%) Fat: 16 g (10%) Calories: 1,500

PART III

CHISELING THE ULTIMATE BODY

chapter 8

CLIMBING THE LADDER OF INTENSITY

Body sculpting has two extremes. At one end, the goal is generating muscle mass. At the other, the focus is fat loss. The middle ground is a combination of the two—a hybrid system. This is a more advanced program that requires a refinement of training techniques to raise the intensity of your workouts.

Before revealing the tricks to turbocharging your workout, let's clarify what intensity actually means. Intensity is defined as the degree of effort or percentage of momentary ability. At the point of muscular failure, 100 percent intensity (effort) is required to complete the last rep. The muscle is pushed to its limit and must contract to its maximum capability to complete the task. Exhausted and disrupted by this demanding stimulus, muscle fibers grow in size.

The question is, can you be sure that all muscle fibers have been recruited and exhausted at the point of failure during that last rep? The answer is probably not. So, is it possible to generate even more intensity and stimulate the muscle further? The answer is yes. You must go beyond failure and step into the zone of higher intensity to ensure that every last muscle fiber is maximally stimulated to the point of exhaustion. The rule of high-intensity training is that the set is just beginning when the muscle fails!

To climb the ladder of intensity, your training techniques must evolve in a positive direction by shifting up a gear to a higher level. There are several ways in which workout intensity can evolve. These methods require manipulating the core elements of your exercise program, namely the resistance, sets, rest intervals, exercise combinations, and the repetition itself. Here are the techniques for intensifying your training.

12 STEPS TO INTENSIFY

The 12 steps up the ladder of intensity are as follows:

1. Increase resistance.
2. Add an exercise.
3. Shorten rest intervals.
4. Prefatigue the muscle.
5. Add super sets.
6. Add drop sets.
7. Change repetition tempo.
8. Use power-paused repetitions.
9. Use partial repetitions.
10. Use static contraction.
11. Add negative reps.
12. Add forced reps.

Step 1: Increase resistance. Gradually increasing the weight you lift intensifies the stimulus that the muscle receives at the point of failure during the last repetition. So if you add an extra 10 pounds (4.5 kg) to your six-rep maximum, your muscles receive a greater stimulus than they did during the previous workout. Added resistance raises the intensity, and the muscle will go beyond its previous point of failure. A larger stimulus provides a bigger challenge for your muscles. As they get stronger, they get bigger. This is the basic theory behind progressive resistance training—as you get stronger, you add more resistance. Aim to add more resistance to each exercise every two to four weeks. A word of caution, however. Your maximum weight is that which you can lift for six repetitions while using perfect form. Performing fewer than six reps of your maximum weight and then trying to add resistance carries a high risk of injury. Only when you're capable of performing 8 to 10 reps on your previous best weight can you safely increase the resistance by 5 percent and try for six reps on the new weight.

Step 2: Add an exercise. Larger muscles groups such as the chest, shoulders, and back benefit from several exercises that target different portions of the muscle. Working the muscle from a different angle intensifies the overall stimulus by bringing additional muscle fibers into action. For instance, a set of flat bench presses performed to failure does not necessarily exhaust the muscle fibers of the upper chest. Add an incline exercise to maximally stimulate the upper (clavicular) portion of the muscle. Similarly, shoulder presses recruit and exhaust the front deltoids, but the lateral (side) and rear heads of the muscle remain relatively underworked. For complete muscular development, all the muscle fibers must be recruited and exhausted in every section of the muscle. Adding additional exercises is a way to ensure maximum intensity for all portions of the muscle. But remember—new movements are required only if you're targeting a separate portion of the muscle. There is little benefit in adding an identical exercise.

Step 3: Shorten rest intervals. The less time you rest between sets and exercises, the more intense the workout becomes. Shortening rest intervals is a safe, effective way to raise intensity. The muscle fibers exhausted by the first set don't have time to recover, so during the second set the muscle must recruit even more fibers to move the resistance. Shortening the interval between sets also burns more calories—a great way to build muscle and burn fat at the same time.

Step 4: Prefatigue the muscle. This technique relates to exercise sequence. It employs an isolation exercise to prefatigue a muscle before moving to a compound movement. This technique aims to recruit and exhaust more muscle fibers, thereby generating a more effective growth response. Performing an isolation exercise exhausts the target muscle so that when you proceed to the compound exercise the fatigued primary muscle will fail before the smaller assistance muscles. For example, perform chest flys to prefatigue the pectorals before performing bench presses. This ensures that the chest muscles fail before the weaker triceps muscles that assist in the pressing movement. You don't want to have to terminate your set of bench presses because the triceps have reached the point of failure before the pectorals. Similarly, preexhausting the deltoid with lateral raises makes the deltoid work harder during shoulder presses, sparing the weaker triceps muscles. I recommend the prefatigue technique as standard practice in focused contraction training (chapter 2), so you should already be using it to good effect.

Step 5: Add super sets. A super set involves performing two exercises back to back without a rest interval. Essentially, this technique takes the prefatigue concept to a higher level of intensity. The difference is that you don't give the muscle time to rest between two exercises. By proceeding immediately to the second set, additional muscle fibers are forced to work after the other fibers have already failed. The second set raises intensity by taking the muscle beyond failure. When you super set two exercises for the same muscle group, the total time under tension increases, and you tap into different muscle fibers as you go from one exercise to the other. This activates a greater percentage of the muscle area, which stimulates extra growth. Examples of super set combinations include leg extensions followed by squats; leg curls followed by stiff-leg deadlifts; chest flys followed by bench presses; deltoid raises followed by shoulder presses; and lat pulldowns followed by rows. If you combine more than two exercises in this way without a rest interval, the sequence becomes a giant set.

Step 6: Add drop sets. A drop set is a method of extending an exercise beyond failure by reducing the weight so that you can perform more reps. When you reach muscular failure at the end of a set, immediately decrease the resistance by 25 to 40 percent and continue the exercise, squeezing out a few more reps until you reach failure with the lowered weight. Rest only for the few seconds it takes to reduce the weight. Drop sets are performed easily on machines where all you need to do is reposition the weight pin to a lower level. During barbell exercises, the plates must be stripped from the bar. For added intensity, do several successive drop sets (double-drop or triple-drop sets) by continuing to reduce the weight each time you reach momentary muscular failure. You can also do drop sets with dumbbells using the down-the-rack technique. Each time the muscle fails, use progressively lighter dumbbells nonstop until the muscles are completely fatigued. This is an excellent method of annihilating the deltoids with dumbbell lateral raises. Let's say your work set fails on the eighth rep with 30-pound (13.6-kg) dumbbells. Proceed immediately down

When performing a drop set with a barbell, have two spotters or training partners remove the extra weight.

the rack to the 20-pound (9-kg) dumbbells, and continue the exercise to failure again. Then drop to the 10-pound (4.5-kg) dumbbells (and so on), continuing the movement until the muscle fails again. By the time you've worked all the way down the rack, it will feel like someone is blow-torching your deltoids!

Step 7: Change repetition tempo. The speed at which you perform a repetition affects intensity. A repetition performed at a fast tempo typically allows the use of a heavier weight, but the rapid acceleration introduces momentum. Excessive momentum with quick repetitions decreases muscle effort. Performing a repetition slowly reduces momentum and maximizes muscle tension throughout the range of motion. Remember that it's the weight (or tension) on the muscle that counts, not the weight on the barbell. Slowing down rep tempo is a method of increasing intensity. This doesn't mean you should use slow-motion reps all the time. On the contrary, varying the rep tempo is the best way to go. Switching from a slow tempo (two seconds down, two seconds up) to a fast tempo (one second down, one second up) taps into different muscle fibers, ensuring maximum muscle recruitment. This effect also is influenced by changing the relative speed of the positive and negative phases of the rep. Slowing the positive phase accentuates the concentric contraction (e.g., two seconds down, four seconds up), whereas doing the negative phase slowly focuses on the eccentric contraction (e.g., four seconds down, two seconds up). To continue adding muscle mass and generating new levels of intensity, the concept of varying rep tempo is very important.

Step 8: Use power-paused repetitions. A paused rep allows you to push past the point of positive muscular failure by providing your muscle with a few seconds' rest in static isometric contraction mode. When you reach muscular failure at the end of a set, hold the weight still for a few seconds. The power pause can be taken at any point during the positive phase of the repetition. Having taken advantage of a few valuable seconds of rest, you'll be able to perform one more complete repetition past the point of failure. Using the paused rep, the set is extended beyond failure in a stop-and-go fashion.

Step 9: Use partial repetitions. By definition, the point of muscular failure occurs when you're no longer able to complete the last repetition through the full range of motion. However, despite not being able to complete a full repetition, the muscle can still perform a partial repetition that employs only a portion of the lift. That shorter arc of motion might involve any part of the repetition—the beginning, midpoint, or end phase. Usually, the partial rep is performed within the range where the muscle is stronger. For instance, a partial rep during a bench press involves the first phase of the lift as the bar is pushed up off the chest. This is the portion where the pectorals generate the most power. Similarly, during shoulder presses, the focus is on the deltoid during the initial phase. With all pressing movements, the triceps do most of the work as your arms approach the lockout position. Rather than quitting when you can no longer complete a full repetition, doing partial reps allows you to take the muscle beyond the point of positive failure.

Step 10: Use static contraction. A static or isometric contraction is the force generated in a muscle when there's no motion and the weight is held still. Because an isometric contraction is stronger than a concentric contraction, it is a means of continuing the set beyond the point of concentric muscular failure. Even though you can no longer lift the weight, your muscle is able to hold the weight static. By squeezing a peak static contraction in the muscle, the muscle is forced to continue working past the point of failure. Hold the weight as long as you can until you reach the point of isometric muscular failure. When the weight finally overcomes the isometric strength, your muscle will be ready to burst.

Step 11: Add negative reps. The strongest phase of a repetition is the negative phase of lowering the weight. Even though the muscle has failed during the positive phase and fatigued during a static contraction, the more powerful eccentric contraction is still able to control the weight as it is lowered. This high-intensity technique uses the strong eccentric (or negative) muscle contraction to perform extra work beyond concentric and isometric muscular failure. The negative rep is performed by lowering the weight down as s-l-o-w-l-y as possible, resisting the pull of gravity. To perform additional negative reps, ask your training partner to lift the weight back up to the top position.

Step 12: Add forced reps. A forced rep is an assisted repetition. When you reach the point of positive muscular failure, your training partner helps you perform another complete repetition by assisting with the lift. Your partner provides just enough help for you to complete another positive phase repetition. This technique allows you to push past the point of positive failure. You'll need an experienced partner to fine-tune the resistance, taking just enough pressure off the bar so that you're forced to work as hard as possible to squeeze out a few extra complete reps.

HYPERINTENSITY TRAINING

"Climbing the ladder" is an apt phrase for stepping up intensity. To go beyond failure, you can take one step at a time or jump several steps together. Intensity is defined as giving 100 percent effort to complete the last repetition to the point of momentary muscular failure. Taking one step up the ladder goes beyond failure, forcing the muscle to recruit extra fibers to generate higher intensity. Jumping several steps up the ladder at once goes beyond the pain to inflict absolute, complete muscular failure, generating hyperintensity.

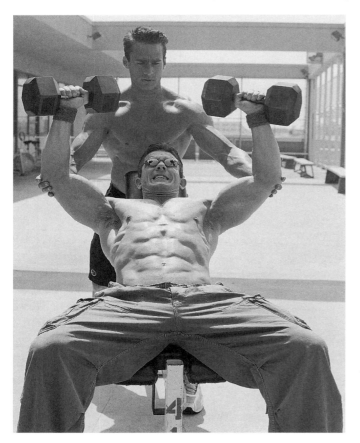

During a forced rep, your training partner will help you squeeze out one more rep.

How does this technique work? Well, let's say you're squeezing out that last rep and you've reached the point of failure. By employing one of the 12 techniques, such as a drop set or some forced reps, you'll go beyond failure into the realm of high intensity. However, if you use several of these advanced techniques together in sequence, such as a static contraction, a negative rep, and a forced rep, you can train past failure over and over again. This brutal multistep system pushes your muscle beyond the pain into the zone of hyperintensity. You've manipulated that final repetition and extended the last set by jumping several steps up the ladder of intensity. Hyperintensity is hardcore. It takes your muscles beyond failure and then some. Your muscles will burn and scream with pain. Give them no mercy. In response to the onslaught of hyperintensity, they'll have no choice but to grow.

So, do you need to use all 12 steps to generate intense workouts? Not necessarily. But the more tricks you have in your gym bag, the more versatile your workouts can become. High-demand techniques such as forced reps and negative reps require the assistance of an experienced training partner. Most of the other methods, such as drop sets and partial reps, can be performed without a spotter, so you can venture into the zone of hyperintensity all by yourself! It's worth mentioning that turning up the intensity is easier (and safer) using machines and dumbbells rather than barbells. If you fail to complete the last rep on most machines, you're safe with or without help.

EXTREME TRAINING

Let's look at some examples to illustrate how to incorporate the brutal tactics of hyperintensity into your workouts. (Just when you thought it was safe to go to the gym!)

Deltoid Demolition

Before you start, warm up your shoulders with a set or two of lateral raises, using a pair of light dumbbells.

The first exercise is dumbbell lateral raises (see page 43). Line up three sets of dumbbells in order of descending weight on the rack, beginning with your eight-repetition maximum weight. For example, if your eight-repetition maximum weight is a pair of 30-pound (13.6-kg) dumbbells, place a pair of 20-pound (9-kg) dumbbells next in line, then a pair of 15-pound (6.8-kg) dumbbells. Grab the heaviest pair of dumbbells and begin doing dumbbell lateral raises in a steady manner (one second up, one second down). When you fail on the eighth rep, hold the dumbbells in a static contraction at the top for as long as you can. Then slowly perform a negative rep, lowering the dumbbells to your sides. Place them back on the rack and immediately grab the next set of dumbbells. Without resting, continue the exercise until you reach failure a second time. Switch dumbbells again, picking up the lightest pair, and resume the exercise. Squeeze those reps out until you reach failure for a third time. Despite the screaming pain in your delts, hold the weight in a static contraction on the last rep for five seconds. Slowly lower the weights to your sides, using a negative rep. Finish with a final blast of partial reps, raising the dumbbells halfway up (about 45 degrees) until you fail for a fourth time.

By this time, your deltoids will be on fire, but you're not done yet. As you catch your breath, head straight for the seated front shoulder press machine. Place the weight pin at your eight-repetition maximum weight and sit down. No need for a warm-up this time—your shoulders are good to go! Squeeze out six to eight reps on the front press to the point of failure. Slowly lower the weight in a negative fashion for a count of five. Then relocate the weight pin, dropping the resistance by about 30 percent, and continue the exercise until you hit failure again. Hold the weight just short of lockout for a count of five in a static contraction. Finally, lower the weight slowly to perform one last negative repetition.

Phew, that's it! Your deltoids are a done deal in under 10 minutes. All you did was two extended sets involving two exercises, but using a combination of hyperintensity techniques, including preexhaustion, drop sets, static contraction, partial reps, and negative reps, your deltoids have been blasted out of orbit. As a result, you inflicted a massive hypertrophic growth response, guaranteed to give you boulder shoulders.

Biceps Blast

All you need to blast your biceps is one extended set of hyperintensity. One of the best exercises to achieve this is the one-arm biceps curl on a preacher bench. The movement can be done using a dumbbell or a machine. With your upper arm supported on the pad the biceps must do all the work. By using one arm at a time, you don't need a training partner to elicit hyperintensity.

First get your biceps into the groove with a light warm-up set. Select a weight equivalent to your six-rep maximum—one arm, remember. Perform the curls in a slow, controlled manner (two seconds up, two seconds down). Once you start to fail, use your free hand to assist in completing an additional six forced repetitions past your failure point. On that final rep, hold the weight in a static peak contraction without assistance for as long as you can. As the isometric contraction begins to fail, perform a negative rep, slowly lowering the weight. When the weight reaches the bottom, use your free hand to lift the weight back up and perform another three negative reps in the same way. By the time you've completed that last negative, your biceps will be bursting at the seams with a pounding muscle pump.

That's all it takes: one extended set taken beyond failure, using a mind-blowing sequence of forced reps, static contraction, and negatives. If you're feeling really masochistic, you can add a drop set, but don't forget your other arm's turn for torture.

Chiseling the Chest

With just two exercises, you can pulverize your pectorals. You'll need to do an isolation exercise to prefatigue the muscle and then a compound, pressing movement. I prefer to start with machine flys, but cable crossovers will also do the trick.

Warm up with one or two light sets before loading the machine with your 8- to 10-rep maximum weight. Focus your mind on the task ahead; once you start the roller coaster, there's no getting off. Begin the set of flys with slow, precise reps. When you hit failure at 8 to 10 reps, reduce the resistance by 30 to 40 percent, and continue the set without rest. Squeeze out as many reps as you can to failure, then drop the weight again by another 30 to 40 percent. Keep pumping out the reps until you fail a third time, then squeeze your hands together in the fully contracted position until you can no longer sustain the static contraction. Let the weight down slowly using a negative rep for a count of five seconds.

By now, your pectoral muscles will be scorching with pain, but the battle ain't over yet. Take a minute to catch your breath and make your way to the Smith machine for incline bench presses. Load the machine with your eight-rep maximum weight and set the backrest at a 30- to 45-degree incline. Perform slow, rhythmic reps until you hit failure, then get your partner to assist for four forced reps. On the last rep, stop short of lockout and hold that bar in a static contraction, squeezing the pecs for five seconds. Perform a slow negative rep, lowering the weight under control toward your chest. Ask your partner to lift the weight back up, then do three more negative reps.

At this point your chest should be annihilated to the point of extreme exhaustion, but if you want more punishment, reduce the weight by 30 to 40 percent and perform a drop set to failure followed by four to six forced reps. That's your hyperintense chest workout.

INTENSITY RULES

Beyond-failure training requires an extreme effort to be generated in an already fatigued muscle. The typical work set is extended and then some. Indeed, when the muscle fails, the set is just beginning. Don't underestimate the exercise-induced assault on your body. Here are a few tips to help you reap the rewards of hyperintensity. Remember: strategy, safety, and recovery.

▶ **Strategy.** The most demanding techniques are forced reps and negative reps performed using your six- to eight-rep maximum weight. Going beyond failure with the maximum possible weight is the ultimate stimulus for gains in mass and strength. However, these extreme techniques demand a high level of caution. Get assistance from a training partner. Taking your maximum weight past failure with forced reps and negative reps should be used sparingly. During these maneuvers, there's a fine line between muscle stimulus and overtraining and injury.

▶ **Safety.** Going beyond failure is less dangerous when you use machines or dumbbells. It's also safer to use a drop set before you perform forced reps or negative reps. Manipulating the repetition is less hazardous after you've gone to failure on a drop set because the weight has been reduced by 30 to 40 percent.

When you climb the ladder of intensity, the risk of injury increases. The well-known bodybuilder's mantra "no pain, no gain" is to an extent true. But the pain you want is a muscular pain, a burning sensation felt deep within the muscle belly that results from muscular fatigue and the build-up of lactic acid inside the tissues. The pain you *don't* want is a sharp, knifelike pain felt in a tendon or joint just before something breaks under excessive strain. Learn to recognize the difference between these two pain sensations. A sharp pain is a warning signal of impending injury—stop the exercise immediately or risk joint or tendon damage.

▶ **Recovery.** The hyperintensity experience is not your typical day at the gym. It's the ultimate challenge, an annihilation of the muscle. As such, this exercise-induced insult requires seven days to repair. If you want to grow from these techniques, you must allow adequate rest for that tortured muscle group to recover between workouts.

chapter 9

ANABOLIC STEROID OVERDRIVE

In the quest for size and strength, many people turn to the dark side of the force, selling their souls to the devil in exchange for an extra inch on their biceps or another plate on their bench press. An estimated one in every three men at an average gym chemically enhances his physique with anabolic steroids, the synthetic drug versions of testosterone.

Many people once believed that steroid use was limited to a few competitive athletes and bodybuilders—those who would risk their health to reach the top of their sport in order to claim titles, financial reward, and fame. This is not the case. Two of every three steroid users are recreational athletes with no intention of competing. The majority of steroid users take these drugs for personal reasons, seeking cosmetic improvement in their physiques. They just want to look good at the gym or buff on the beach.

The majority of steroid users are 20 to 40 years of age, but 10 percent of users are teens. Surveys indicate that 2 to 5 percent of high school students are using these drugs. The steroid habit can start at a young age and continue for 10 years or more.

STEROID ACTION

Testosterone, the active ingredient in steroids, has two effects on the body: anabolic and androgenic. Testosterone's anabolic action builds body tissue by increasing lean muscle mass and bone density and reducing body fat. It ensures a positive nitrogen balance by stimulating protein synthesis and improving protein use. Testosterone's androgenic actions are responsible for the so-called secondary sex characteristics that turn boys into men. All those changes that occur to boys during puberty—voice deepening, oily skin, growth of body and facial hair, development of male sex organs, and increased sex drive—occur because of a surge in teenage testosterone. A young adult male produces about 10 milligrams of testosterone each day, approximately 70 milligrams per week. The concentration of testosterone circulating in the blood is normally 300 to 1,000 nanograms per deciliter (ng/dl). The average level for adult men is about 500 ng/dl.

When discussing steroid doses, a distinction must be made between therapeutic doses aimed at restoring normal testosterone levels and the so-called supraphysiological doses used nonmedically for muscle building. The weekly dose for testosterone replacement is about 100 milligrams. According to scientific data, a weekly dose of at least 300 milligrams of testosterone is required for muscle building. This dose is equivalent to the combined testosterone levels of several men. Hence the term supraphysiological—more than the normal amount.

The results of recent scientific studies on testosterone are interesting. First, a 600-milligram weekly dose of testosterone enanthate taken over a 10-week period produces a gain of 14 pounds in fat-free muscle mass and a 40 percent increase in strength. Second, testosterone-induced increases in muscle size are a result of muscle fiber hypertrophy, with an increase in the cross-sectional area of the muscle fibers. Third, these anabolic effects are dose-dependant. Smaller doses of testosterone—125 milligrams per week or less—do not elevate the body's testosterone above normal levels. Only when the weekly dose of steroids is above 300 milligrams per week does the testosterone level climb above the normal range. A weekly 300-milligram dose triples the average testosterone level, and a weekly 600-milligram dose elevates the level up to six times the normal value. As a result, the 600-milligram dose almost doubles the muscle fiber cross-sectional area, thereby increasing muscle size.

Testosterone exerts this anabolic effect by acting directly on the muscle itself. The hormone binds to androgen receptors in the muscle cell, switching on protein synthesis and inducing muscle growth. Testosterone also has several complementary anabolic actions elsewhere in the body. It stimulates the release of growth hormone and exerts an anticatabolic effect that slows protein breakdown. Testosterone also has a behavioral effect on the brain that might positively influence training intensity, thus increasing muscle strength.

As a result of recent research efforts, testosterone is now being prescribed as medical treatment for AIDS-related wasting disorders and as hormone-replacement therapy in elderly men with low testosterone (the so-called male andropause). Testosterone has also been found to speed up the healing of muscle contusion injury and alleviate symptoms of depression in men.

STEROID DOSES AND REGIMENS

When it comes to discussing muscle-building steroid regimens, there's one big problem—the information is not based on scientific clinical investigation. Underground steroid dose regimes are anecdotal, based on word-of-mouth testimonies. In the absence of medical guidance, steroid users have been left to their own devices. Drug doses and regimens have been developed through trial and error, passed down by veteran users or through underground steroid manuals written by self-proclaimed steroid gurus.

So what's going on behind the closed doors of the locker room? A few years ago, I carried out a survey of the anabolic steroid regimens of 100 male steroid users. The results revealed that steroid doses ranged from 250 to 3,200 milligrams per week. The majority of users (88 percent) administered less than 1,000 milligrams of steroids per week. Some bodybuilders who chose to be precise with their doses calculated them using this formula: one milligram of steroid per kilogram of body weight per day. To achieve these megadoses, most users combined two or more types of steroid, a process known as "stacking."

Steroids tend to be used in cycles lasting from 4 to 12 weeks. Regular steroid users allow a 4- to 6-week gap between cycles to clear the system. Approximately half of the study group stated that their total annual steroid use amounted to more than six months each year. A handful of bodybuilders admitted to continuous steroid use for 52 weeks of the year without ever coming off the drugs.

In my survey, the most popular drug used was Nandrolone decanoate (used by over 80 percent), followed by injectable testosterones, such as Sustenon 250. Dianabol tablets came in third. A combination of injectable and oral steroids was used by 85 percent of this group, 11 percent used injectable drugs exclusively, and 4 percent used tablets only. In other words, the vast majority (96 percent) of steroid users choose intramuscular injections. Sample self-administered steroid regimens of new and veteran users, as reported during the survey, are shown in table 9.1.

Drug use by steroid users is not confined to anabolic steroids. Apparently, 9 out of 10 steroid users have a polypharmaceutical palate, taking a mix of muscle-shaping drugs in addition to stacking different brands of steroids. These steroid-accessory drugs are used for a variety of reasons and can be grouped according to their desired effect.

Thermogenic fat-burning drugs such as clenbutarol, ephedrine, and thyroid hormone are common among steroid users. Nonsteroid anabolic agents such as growth hormone and insulin are gaining in popularity, particularly among

TABLE 9.1

Sample Steroid Regimes (Self-Administered)

Cycle	Steroids	Dosage	Method of delivery	Time frame
Novice	Dianabol Nandrolone decanoate	25 mg/day 200 mg/week	Oral Injection	4 to 6 weeks
Mass	Sustenon Nandrolone decanoate	500 mg/week 400 mg/week	Injection Injection	4 to 6 weeks
Cutting	Testosterone propionate Nandrolone decanoate Stanozolol	300 mg/week 400 mg/week 150 mg/week	Injection Injection Injection	4 to 6 weeks
Off				4 weeks

competitive bodybuilders. Diuretics are used in an attempt to flush out subcutaneous body water prior to competition, and peculiar products such as Synthol are injected into lagging body parts to improve muscle symmetry and proportion. Medication also is taken to reduce side effects associated with steroid use. For example, the antiestrogen drug Tamoxifen (Nolvadex) is used to prevent or treat steroid-induced gynecomastia. Human chorionic gonadotrophin (HCG) is sometimes used to kick-start suppressed endogenous testosterone at the end of a steroid cycle to minimize muscle loss and withdrawal symptoms during the off cycle.

Many of these steroid accessory drugs are potentially more dangerous than the steroids themselves. The unsupervised use of insulin, diuretics, and thyroxine can precipitate a number of medical emergencies. It's a worrisome trend that healthy young bodybuilders take more drugs than their elderly grandparents with multiple medical ailments.

STEROID SIDE EFFECTS AND HEALTH RISKS

Because of their potential health risks, anabolic steroids are classed as illegal drugs and banned by many sporting organizations. The fact is that testosterone, the active ingredient in anabolic steroids, *does* work. It boosts muscle mass and turbocharges your sex drive. The problem is that testosterone, like any other drug, has potentially harmful effects.

How dangerous are these drugs? Are we to believe the shocking media reports of steroid-related deaths and the scare tactics employed by health professionals? If steroids are so dangerous, how come thousands of bodybuilders use them? Let's examine the hazards of steroid use in more detail.

There are many potential side effects associated with anabolic and androgenic steroids. Testosterone's anabolic action builds muscle, but its androgenic properties can adversely affect several body systems, including the cardiovascular, hormonal, reproductive, gastrointestinal, and nervous systems, as well as the skin. I've scanned the medical literature and compiled a list of all the possible complications of anabolic steroids. Take a look at table 9.2 for a summary of what can go wrong.

So, if you take anabolic steroids, what are the odds of developing a complication? The answer isn't straightforward because many factors determine the frequency and severity of side effects. In several short-term medical studies, a 600-milligram weekly dose of testosterone caused no serious side effects in healthy adult men. Although this is a revelation in terms of steroid safety, we must interpret the data with caution. First, the studies lasted less than three months. Second, a 600-milligram dose is moderate in comparison to what many bodybuilders use, often over long periods. One thing we do know is that the bigger the dose and the longer the duration of steroid use, the greater the health risk.

Out of the 100 steroid users in my survey, only 12 denied any side effects. This means that 88 percent of them experienced some kind of steroid-related complication. In other words, at least four of every five steroid users reported unwanted symptoms. These data imply that if you take large doses of anabolic steroids on a regular basis, your chance of experiencing a side effect is 80 percent or greater.

The bottom line is that anabolic steroid users have an 80 percent chance of experiencing at least one of these common complications: acne, gynecomastia, testicle shrinkage, stretch marks, fluctuating sex drive, withdrawal symptoms, or drug dependence.

You might be thinking that these common steroid-induced complications are not real side effects—they're nothing more than a minor inconvenience. In fact, most steroid users accept these problems as necessary evils in the pursuit of size, and rather than quit using steroids, they use other drugs to combat the unwanted symptoms. Some of the problems are reversible and disappear when steroid use is discontinued. Other effects, such as hair loss, stretch marks, and acne scars, can be permanent.

▶ **Testicle shrinkage.** When you use anabolic steroids, your body senses a testosterone overload, and your testes stop making testosterone. Like many other body tissues, the testes function on the "use it or lose it" principle. When they're out of work, they shrink in size (atrophy). So while you're stomping around the mall trying on new oversized shirts and baggy pants, you might also have

TABLE 9.2

Negative Effects of Anabolic Steroids

General
Acne
Gynecomastia
Stretch marks
Fluid retention (edema)
Male-pattern baldness
Increased facial and body hair
Testicular shrinkage
Decreased sperm count
Fluctuating sex drive
High blood pressure
Raised cholesterol
Liver toxicity
Prostate enlargement
Hormone suppression
Mood swings ("'roid rage")
Addiction or dependence
Withdrawal symptoms
Injection-related
Pain
Bruising
Scar tissue
Infection or abscess
Nerve injury
HIV or hepatitis (needle sharing)
Legislation (USA)
Schedule 3 controlled substance

to purchase a multipack of extra small underwear. The only way to halt this period of self-induced testicular unemployment is to stop using steroids. Your testes will eventually regain their original size, but it will take six months or more of being steroid free. Some steroid users try to expedite this process by using such drugs as human chorionic gonadotrophin (Pregnyl) or clomiphene citrate (Clomid). These fertility drugs can kick-start sleeping testes back into action, but the effect is only temporary. The bottom line is that if you toy with testosterone, your testicles get tiny. You can't use juice and have a handful of big nuts at the same time.

▶ **Gynecomastia.** The development of excessive breast tissue affects one in three male steroid users. What happens is that some of that extra testosterone circulating through your body gets converted to the hormone estrogen, which can lead to the development of a couple of female appendages. For many steroid users, this side effect is reversible—when they quit using the drugs, the gynecomastia disappears—but this isn't always the case. Treatment for gynecomastia is the antiestrogen drug tamoxifen (Nolvadex), 20 milligrams daily. This prescription-only medication can be used to treat gynecomastia or prevent it from occurring in the first place. Persistent cases of gynecomastia that resist drug treatment usually require surgical excision.

▶ **Skin changes.** Testosterone is converted into dihydrotestosterone (DHT), a by-product that makes the skin more oily, which causes acne. DHT can also accelerate male-pattern baldness. The prescription drug finasteride (Propecia or Proscar) might help block the conversion of testosterone to DHT. Steroids can also affect skin elasticity, inflicting stretch marks as the muscles balloon in size.

▶ **Withdrawal.** Steroid-induced problems don't end when you finish a steroid cycle. At least 70 percent of steroid users report symptoms of withdrawal after quitting the drug. Withdrawal symptoms include loss of muscle size and strength, fatigue, reduced sex drive, and depression. Because steroids suppress your own hormone production, when you discontinue the drugs your testosterone level drops into your boots. That is, coming off the juice leaves you with the testosterone level of a toddler. It's no surprise that you feel as weak as a kitten when you stop taking steroids. Your muscles shrink, your strength falls off, and you lose interest in sex.

▶ **Addiction.** The knee-jerk reaction to withdrawal is to score some more steroids pretty damn quick. You crave the rush of all that testosterone pumping through your veins, and this does represent a form of psychological (and physical) drug dependence. Sure, it's tough pedaling a bicycle to the gym when you're used to driving a tank—but you've got to step down sometime or risk devastating consequences.

People once thought that anabolic steroids damaged tendons. Recent scientific evidence has shown this is not true. Anabolic steroids do not damage or weaken tendons. These drugs can make tendons mechanically stiffer and less elastic, but similar changes are induced in tendons by regular exercise. Anabolic steroids neither reduce tendon strength nor inflict any significant biochemical or anatomical alterations in tendon tissue. A word of caution, though. Anabolic steroids can increase muscular strength dramatically within a few weeks. Tendons, meanwhile, require longer to adapt (because they have a poorer blood supply). To avoid tendon injury, increase weight gradually to allow tendons time to get stronger.

STEROID STICKS: INJECTION ISSUES

That guy at the gym who's the size of a gorilla might be big and strong, but don't congratulate him with a pat on the butt after his 600-pound bench press because his ass hurts from all those steroid needles. Needle stick injections are a big part of the steroid game. Nine of 10 steroid users inject muscle-building drugs; along with all those needle sticks comes a selection of injection-related problems.

Like most drugs, anabolic steroids can be taken by mouth or delivered via intramuscular injection. Tablets are a convenient way of taking medications—you simply pop them in your mouth and swallow. By contrast, injectable drugs require a needle, a syringe, and a sharp stick.

The side effects of steroids are similar for both tablet and injectable versions of the drug. Generally speaking, the health risks are predominantly dose-related— the bigger the dose, the greater the risk. However, tablets and injections differ slightly when it comes to complications.

Tablets are potentially more harmful to the liver. Any oral drug absorbed from the gut passes through the liver before it's distributed elsewhere in the body. When taken in large doses by mouth, tablet versions of anabolic steroids can upset liver function. For this reason, many steroid users choose injectable forms of the drug to minimize toxic effects on the liver. Injectable versions of the drug are placed into muscle and released directly into the bloodstream, bypassing the liver. This means that larger doses can be injected without the liver taking a big hit. But there's a trade-off. Although the liver is partly spared drug toxicity, sticking a needle into your body is not without risk, especially if the person giving the injection has not been trained to perform the procedure. Injection problems are unrelated to the type of drug inside the syringe. They are purely the result of the needle stick. Common side effects of poor injection technique are pain, bruising, scar tissue build-up, nerve injury, infection or abscess, and HIV or hepatitis from sharing needles.

Intramuscular injection inflicts two forms of pain. The first is that sharp stick as the needle penetrates the skin. The second is a deep discomfort as the injection pushes the muscle fibers apart, creating a little pocket of fluid. The larger the volume of fluid, the greater the pain. Bigger muscles such as the buttocks and thighs can comfortably accommodate two to three milliliters of fluid. In smaller muscles, such as the shoulders, one milliliter is about the maximal limit of comfort. The fluid disappears as the drug is absorbed, but the site remains slightly damaged and inflamed from the needle stick for a while longer. If you inject into the same site within the space of a few days, you can cause a double jeopardy situation. Double the fluid, double the damage, double the pain.

Needle size also influences the amount of pain. Larger diameter needles cause more damage than narrower ones. Needle diameter in millimeters is called the gauge. The larger the gauge, the finer the needle is in thickness. Obviously, finer needles cause less tissue damage, but the narrower the needle, the more difficult it is to push the fluid through. The viscosity of oil-based steroids is too thick to pass through tiny needles. As a rule, oil-based steroids can be injected with a 22-gauge (0.7 millimeter) needle, and less viscous water-based steroids can be delivered through smaller (23- or 25-gauge) needles. To improve comfort and safety with regular injections, it's better to use the smallest needle possible. The length of needle is also important. A 1-1/2-inch needle is required to deliver a deep intramuscular injection into larger muscles, such as the buttocks. Shorter 5/8-inch or 1/2-inch needles can be used to inject smaller muscles. If you sink a 2-inch needle into a small muscle, you're likely to hit an underlying nerve or blood vessel.

Every time a needle pierces muscle, a small amount of bleeding occurs. Under normal circumstances, this is not a problem, but if the needle hits a blood vessel, blood loss into the surrounding tissue can cause an unsightly (and painful) bruise or hematoma. Much worse, injecting the drug directly into the bloodstream can cause a life-threatening embolism, stroke, or cardiac arrest. An injection site bruise does not usually require treatment but takes a week or so to heal. Bruising can be minimized by applying direct pressure on the injection site using a cotton swab or facial tissue. Keep pressing for a minute or two until you're sure that the bleeding has stopped.

An injection needle actually damages muscle. As the stick plunges inside, it inflicts a tiny hole that heals by forming a scar. A small slither of scar tissue from one injection is no big deal, but repeated needle sticks eventually create a large area of scarring. Subsequent injections into this hard, gritty stuff becomes difficult and painful. Many bodybuilders don't realize that scar tissue is not normal muscle tissue; it doesn't contract or flex. It just sits there in the muscle like a golf ball.

To minimize scar tissue build-up, reduce the number of injections into the same area by rotating injection sites. Employing an injection site rota means using a different site each time you inject, thereby avoiding injecting into the same area for at least a week or two. To illustrate this point, let's assume that you required regular intramuscular injections for a legitimate medical reason. The qualified technician would select a different injection site each time. For example: injection 1 into the right buttock, injection 2 into the left buttock, injection 3 into the right thigh, injection 4 into the left thigh, injection 5 into the right buttock again, and so on.

Some bodybuilders attempt to fix holes in their physiques with a zap of oil. Injecting muscles with products such as Synthol gives an illusion of size but does not induce muscle growth. The fake size isn't muscle tissue—it's a bubble of oil, an injectable implant. Site injection with Synthol—a practice I call "spot welding"—is a temporary fix. The spot weld doesn't contract. The muscle tissue becomes inflamed, eventually forming a bump of scar tissue that resembles a tumor of mutant muscle.

It's scary how bodybuilders play their own version of Russian roulette with steroid injections, blindly stabbing different body parts without knowing the location of nerves and blood vessels. Site injection is a common practice by bodybuilders. Steroids are injected directly into lagging muscle groups to induce a localized increase in size. The problem is most muscles are intimately adjacent to nerves, blood vessels, and other important anatomical structures. For instance, the radial nerve lies immediately under the triceps horseshoe, the sciatic nerve passes under the lower portion of your gluteals, and the axillary nerve lies beneath the deltoid muscle. If your misplaced needle hits an artery or vein, the extra blood loss creates a good-sized bruise. Striking a nerve with your needle feels like an electric shock. The damaged nerve can result in loss of feeling and muscle weakness.

So what are the safest injection sites? If you read the medical texts, you'll learn that the three commonly used safe sites for administering intramuscular injections are the upper outer quadrant of the buttocks, the outer aspect of the middle to upper thigh, and the outer portion of the shoulder.

Another possible side effect of poor injection technique is infection, which usually results from accidental contamination of a sterile needle, reusing needles, or sharing injection equipment or multidose vials with another person. All injections should be given using a sterile technique in a clean environment without contaminating the end of the needle. The locker room of your local gym does not qualify as a sterile area! Cleansing the skin with an alcohol swab can reduce the risk of infection. If the needle does get dirty after being removed from the sterile packaging, you run the risk of introducing a bacterial infection under your skin. This infection can develop into an abscess filled with pus, which usually needs to be lanced or surgically removed. Fake or counterfeit steroids that have not undergone proper sterilization can also increase the risk of bacterial infection. A more serious infection complication can arise from sharing needles. This hazardous practice risks the transmission of the HIV virus and hepatitis B or C.

Although short-term use of low doses of testosterone appears relatively safe, the potential health risks of long-term steroid use are still being researched. As the dose and duration of steroid use escalates, so do the health risks. Relatively minor side effects evolve into bigger problems, manifesting as irreparable heart or liver damage, high blood pressure, stroke, or heart attack.

If everybody jumped off a cliff, would you follow them? Self-administering anabolic steroids is illegal and dangerous. As with any drug, there's use, and there's abuse. The old saying "everything in moderation" surely applies here.

The chances are good that at least one in three readers of this book have used anabolic steroids. If you choose to use these drugs, stick with lower doses and take adequate off cycles. Remember that bodybuilding is supposed to be a healthy pastime, not a fast track to an early demise. In the next chapter, we'll look at some of the nutritional supplements that offer a safe method of enhancing your physique.

10

SUPER SUPPLEMENT STACK

In the same way that your exercise regime evolves by climbing the ladder of intensity, your fuel intake can evolve with supplementation. However, keep the need for nutritional supplements in perspective. As the name suggests, these products are intended to supplement a balanced diet. They don't replace the need for food, nor do they compensate for a poor diet. Nevertheless, consuming the right food and the best supplements will improve efforts at muscle gain and fat loss. Enhancing your physique with nutritional supplements is a safer choice than chemical assistance with anabolic steroids.

The idea that certain substances enhance sporting performance is not new. In fact, the notion dates back to the first Olympic games in 776 B.C. Historical records describe some athletes using herbs and plant extracts to gain a competitive edge. Not so long ago, a "protein shake" meant a glass of whole milk with a few raw eggs thrown in. Over the past few decades, we have witnessed major developments in sports nutrition. Health food stores have become as commonplace as coffee shops, and the catalog of different products can be confusing. New must-have products are emerging so fast, it's tough to keep up.

Over the years, I have witnessed many products come and go. New supplements get hyped as the next best thing, only to disappear without a trace by your next birthday. Sadly, the quality of some supplements is questionable. We've all seen those amazing advertising claims that seem too good to be true. It's tough for consumers to distinguish fact from fiction, and we should not have to spend hours scanning the medical literature to determine whether a company's research claims are bogus. It isn't right that consumers are misled into parting with hard-earned cash for an overpriced product that is no more effective than powdered milk, particularly if that supplement could cause more harm than good.

If I were to list the thousands of products available on the market today, you'd have to sift through a compendium the size of a phone book. Instead, in this chapter I'll narrow my discussion to the supplements I believe are most useful for muscle building and fat loss.

There are six common reasons for using nutritional supplements:

1. To conveniently boost calories. Supplements are ready to eat anytime, anywhere.
2. To add fuel and increase protein intake.
3. To gain an ergogenic edge, boosting your workout performance.
4. To help burn fat and lose weight.
5. To provide a hormonal boost and help anabolism.
6. To provide additional benefits, such as preventing joint pain or vitamin deficiency.

As I mentioned, nutritional aids are intended to supplement your diet, not replace it. None of the products listed in this chapter is absolutely essential, but all of them can help build muscle and support fat loss. Based on efficacy and safety, the products currently available for bodybuilding purposes are summarized in table 10.1.

I have put together a short list of the most effective supplements on the market today. Each product has qualified for inclusion based on its track record and scientific research. But keep two points in mind. First, the list contains only products that can help you build muscle and lose fat *legally*. I have not included products that are illegal or those not backed by scientific research. Nor have I included products that have other potential benefits such as improved sexual performance, restful sleep, or a reduced risk of colds and flu. This book is all about sculpting a better body, so the supplements are streamlined to this topic. Second, science is constantly moving forward. In the near future, new products will be added to this list. The ones listed here are the best supplements legally available at the time I am writing this chapter.

For convenience, for each product I'll answer the same four questions: What is it? Does it work? How much should I take? Is it safe?

TABLE 10.1

Doctor's Bag of Supplements

Supplement	Comments
Meal-replacement products	Convenient source of nutrients. Useful when you don't have time to prepare (or eat) a meal.
Whey protein	Excellent source of quality protein to boost daily intake. Liquid formulations are easily digested and absorbed, making them ideal for refueling immediately after a workout.
Creatine	Enhances exercise performance and recovery. Increases muscle size and strength.
Fat burners	Effective means of losing weight and increasing energy.
Pro-hormones	Steroid precursors that convert to testosterone.
Glucosamine	Natural alternative to anti-inflammatory medication in the treatment and prevention of joint pain.
Multivitamins/minerals	Although vitamins and minerals will not directly help you build muscle or lose fat, supplementation ensures that you avoid dietary deficiencies.

MEAL-REPLACEMENT PRODUCTS

A meal-replacement product (MRP) does exactly what its name suggests. It provides a convenient way for you to consume all the nutrients you'd expect from a complete, healthy meal. The main advantage of a good MRP is convenience. It can be consumed anytime, anywhere, with minimal preparation. What's more, when you're outside of the home, you don't have to rely on traditional fast-food eateries, where the calorie content of the meal is an unknown quantity. The product label of a good quality meal replacement tells you exactly what you're eating. MRPs are also generally cheaper than your average fast-food meal.

A good MRP should provide nutrients in the proportions you need, such as 50 percent protein, 40 percent carbohydrates, and 10 percent fat. It should also contain all the essential vitamins and minerals. The difference between a good bodybuilding MRP and other formulations is the relative content of protein and fat. Try to choose a product containing at least 30 grams of protein with no more than a few grams of fat. Match the calorie content of the meal replacement with what you would expect from a regular meal—around 300 calories. MRPs are available in powder form (mixed with water), in ready-to-drink bottles, or in bars that look like candy bars.

MRPs are a reliable source of fast, convenient food. They are not directly ergogenic; they won't boost your workout performance. They will, however, enhance recovery by providing all the essential muscle-building nutrients. The liquid formulation is easily digested and more readily absorbed than a meal of solid food, so you won't feel bloated though your hunger will be satisfied.

Depending on your daily schedule, you can substitute an MRP for any meal. You should consume at least three meals of solid food each day, but an MRP is ideal for either of the other two meals, typically eaten at midmorning or mid-afternoon. As long as your MRP is from a reputable manufacturer, there's no cause for health concerns, but do make sure it's not loaded with fat calories.

PROTEIN

Protein is a large molecule made of amino acids. It's a component of all living cells and is essential for the growth and repair of body tissues. Protein is rich in nitrogen and thus controls the body's nitrogen content. A positive nitrogen balance is necessary to provide the anabolic environment you need for muscle growth.

Protein is an essential nutrient for building muscle. As a rule, try to consume at least one gram of protein per pound of body weight each day. This means that each of your five or six daily meals should contain a portion of protein.

Although protein is found in a variety of foods, some types of protein are better for building muscle than others. Every source of protein has a biological value (BV) that determines its quality in terms of digestion, absorption, and muscle-building benefit. The higher the BV, the more effective the protein is for muscle growth. The following are the BVs for some popular sources of protein: soy protein (74), chicken (79), beef (80), tuna fish (83), and egg whites (88). Although these foods are excellent sources of protein, preparing them can be inconvenient, and making them tasty sometimes means adding unwanted calories.

Protein supplementation is a convenient way of increasing your intake and ensuring you get your daily requirement of amino acids. The most effective muscle-building supplements contain whey protein, which has a BV of over 100. To make protein supplements even more convenient, some products are packaged ready to drink or are available in the form of tasty protein bars.

To meet your daily protein requirement, each of your meals should contain at least 30 grams of protein. Your intestine will absorb 30 to 40 grams of protein per meal. If you want to stay lean, make sure your protein supplement is not loaded with extra carbohydrates or calories.

Consuming 30 to 40 grams of protein with each meal is not harmful if you have good kidney function and you stay well hydrated.

CREATINE

Creatine is high-grade muscle fuel. After exercise, the muscle's supply of creatine depletes, and it can take days to replenish the fuel store. Dietary supplementation with creatine boosts energy stores in muscle, enhancing recovery and exercise performance.

Creatine is the best legal supplement for gaining muscle mass and strength. In a recent review of scientific studies involving sports supplements, creatine came out on top of the list. Creatine has more research data documenting its ergogenic effects than any other product on the market at this time. If you want the best bang for your buck, creatine is the supplement of choice.

Expect to gain up to 10 pounds of muscle and increase your strength by 10 percent within several weeks of supplementing your diet with creatine. Creatine creates these results by enhancing energy stores in muscle, boosting muscle cell volume, increasing protein synthesis, and stimulating the release of growth hormone. As a result, exercise capability is improved, and recovery time is quicker. Gains in muscle size and strength are better when creatine is combined with whey protein, and the improvements are maintained for six weeks after supplementation is discontinued.

Consume a loading dose of 25 grams daily for the first three to five days, followed by a maintenance dose of five grams per day. With supplementation, the concentration of creatine is elevated by about 25 percent. This value reaches a peak after one week, indicating that the creatine level has reached a plateau. Once the fuel tank is full, consuming larger doses won't provide additional benefit. You can take your daily dose of creatine at any time during the day, but for the best effect, take it within an hour after your workout to take advantage of the anabolic window.

Most scientific studies have praised creatine's safety record, concluding that short-term use of this supplement is well tolerated in healthy young adults. However, creatine ingestion has been reported to cause cramps, dehydration, dizziness, stomach upset, and kidney problems. The main safety concern is that creatine possibly upsets the body's fluid balance, placing unwanted stress on the kidneys and liver. This remains a theoretical risk, however, because safety tests on creatine have failed to demonstrate adverse effects. Overall, it appears that creatine does not cause harm to healthy young adults who use the recommended dosage. To ensure safety, it's wise to cycle your creatine use. For example, take it for 6 to 12 weeks, then go off it for 4 to 6 weeks to allow your body to return to normal. Creatine supplementation is not recommended in children, the elderly, or people with medical disorders.

FAT BURNERS

Supplements that promote fat loss are commonly called fat burners, thermogenic supplements, or lipotropic agents. These products can increase the body's natural fat burning potential. They work via a process called thermogenesis, causing a natural elevation in your metabolic rate, allowing you to burn more calories while at rest. The more calories burned, the greater the weight loss.

Most fat burners combine the thermogenic properties of several ingredients, usually ephedrine, caffeine, and aspirin (known as the ECA stack). For a more natural approach to fat loss, many products contain the herbal equivalents of ECA, namely ma-huang (ephedra), guarana (caffeine), and willow bark (aspirin or salicin). Because of safety concerns regarding ephedra, there is a move toward newer fat-loss supplements that are ephedra-free.

Fat loss from ECA is likely the result of a combination of effects, including increased metabolic rate, raised body temperature, suppressed appetite, improved use of fats for energy, and greater exercise intensity. Ephedrine is a thermogenic agent that can convert excess calories into heat instead of fat. It also suppresses appetite. Caffeine promotes the use of fatty acids as an energy source during exercise so you can train harder longer. It also has a mild diuretic effect, which helps shed excess water, making the body appear leaner and tighter. Besides their fat-burning properties, both ephedrine and caffeine are stimulants that increase alertness, helping you exercise with greater intensity. Aspirin works in concert with ephedrine and caffeine to prolong the fat-burning effects in the body. Scientific studies indicate that the combination of 20 milligrams of ephedrine with 200 milligrams of caffeine and 15 milligrams of aspirin optimizes fat loss. Other natural extracts that enhance fat oxidation and suppress appetite include hydroxycitric acid (garcinia) and green tea. Fat-loss agents work best when combined with a low-calorie, low-fat diet and regular aerobic exercise.

The combinations of ingredients in fat-burning products vary, and the serving size of individual brands is different. Read the product label and follow dosage instructions carefully. Start with the smallest serving size to monitor your own individual tolerance of the active ingredients. The maximum dose of ephedrine for a healthy adult is 20 milligrams per serving, with no more than 100 milligrams in a 24-hour period. Fat-burners containing ephedra should not be used continuously for more than 12 weeks. If you're worried about the risks of ephedra-based products, consult your physician beforehand or use an ephedra-free fat burner.

The potential side effects of fat burners arise from the stimulant effects of ephedrine and caffeine. Unwanted symptoms include headache, sleeplessness, tremor, anxiety, dizziness, irregular heart beat, behavioral changes, and high blood pressure. Despite this unpleasant list of symptoms, research on the use of herbal ephedra-caffeine ingestion for weight loss has demonstrated no serious side effects in healthy subjects during a six-month period. However, I want to emphasize that fat burners containing ephedra are intended for use by healthy adults. These products are not suitable for people who suffer from medical conditions including (but not limited to) high blood pressure, irregular heart beat, recurrent headaches, stroke, diabetes, bleeding disorders, psychiatric diseases, or stomach ulcers. Fat burners made by reputable companies will have a statement clearly warning consumers on the product label. Some people react more strongly to ephedra and caffeine than others, and there is an individual susceptibility to adverse effects. If you suffer any unusual symptoms while using a fat burner, discontinue use and consult your doctor. Because of these health risks, over-the-counter sale of ephedra is illegal in many countries. A safer way to promote fat loss is to use ephedra-free products.

PRO-HORMONES

Steroid pro-hormones such as androstenedione, norandrostenedione, and dehydroepiandrosterone (DHEA) are precursors or building blocks for testosterone. When consumed, pro-hormones convert to testosterone inside your body. In theory, these supplements are a natural method of increasing testosterone levels. At the time of writing, these products are legally available without prescription at health food stores. However, because of safety issues, steroid pro-hormones might be withdrawn from the shelves sometime in the near future.

Research indicates that a 300-milligram dose of the pro-hormone androstenedione can increase testosterone levels. However, whether this effect benefits muscle size and strength is not yet proven. The recommended dose of androstenedione is 300 milligrams daily. Lower doses do not raise testosterone levels.

Pro-hormones are not free of potential problems. First, there's the issue of safety. Research studies investigating the effects of androstenedione given to healthy adult men in daily doses of 300 milligrams for up to 12 weeks have found the product to be relatively safe. However, concerns exist that pro-hormones produce side effects similar to anabolic steroids, such as acne. The ingested pro-hormone can also convert into the female steroid estrogen, and some male users have developed gynecomastia (female breast tissue). For women, there's a risk of developing masculine features (hirsuitism), and in children there's a possibility of stunted growth. A second problem relates to drug testing. If you're taking pro-hormones, your urine might test positive for anabolic steroids.

GLUCOSAMINE

Glucosamine is a naturally occurring amino-sugar, which plays an important role in the cartilage that cushions human joints. Glucosamine is a building block for the large molecules that attract and hold water inside cartilage, providing better shock absorption. Unfortunately, cartilage wears down over time, and the body's ability to replace it slows or ceases. This can result in arthritis and painful, stiff joints. Glucosamine acts as a joint saver, helping maintain the cartilage cushion and lubrication inside your joints, much like oiling the moving parts of a machine.

As your body gets older, the cartilage cushion inside your joints wears down. The process is similar to tire wear as the mileage on your vehicle increases. Over time, lifting heavy weights can injure joints and increase the rate of cartilage loss.

Glucosamine supplementation may help reduce the risk of developing joint pain.

As the years go by, glucosamine supplementation may help slow down the wear and tear inside your joints as well as help relieve symptoms of joint pain.

The recommended dose of glucosamine is 1,500 milligrams daily. The benefit of other additives, such as chondoitin, is unproven at this time.

Based on current scientific knowledge, glucosamine supplementation is safe. Few side effects have been reported with glucosamine use. Because it's a naturally occurring substance, it's less toxic than other drugs used to treat joint pain and arthritis.

MULTIVITAMINS AND MINERALS

Vitamins and minerals are essential dietary micronutrients. They serve many functions in the body, and dietary deficiency can result in ill health. These micronutrients don't directly help build muscle or reduce body fat, but an adequate supply of dietary vitamins and minerals is necessary for optimal athletic performance (see chapter 6).

A well-balanced diet provides all the vitamins and minerals you need. If you suspect your diet is not consistently well balanced, a simple solution to avoid deficiency is to take a daily multivitamin and mineral supplement. There are many inexpensive multivitamin and mineral formulations available at most health food and drug stores. Usually, one tablet per day provides the recommended daily intake of all the essential micronutrients—just be sure to check the label carefully.

GOODIES OR GIMMICKS?

Here are a few tips on how to distinguish good supplements from bad and effective nutritional aids from fads.

▶ **Tip 1.** Select brands made by a reputable company with a track record in sports nutrition. Larger companies that have been in the business for many years are more likely to produce legitimate products than are smaller, relatively new companies.

▶ **Tip 2.** Be cautious of new products that emerge overnight and claim to be the next best thing. It takes years of clinical research to prove the benefit of new products.

▶ **Tip 3.** Beware of advertising claims that appear too good to be true. Frequently, the references cited in these ads don't exist. If the name of the scientific journal is abbreviated beyond recognition or if the reference is not written in English, there's a good chance the source is fictitious. Another suspicious feature is when the research was not performed on humans. It's just not possible to predict the effect a product will have on human subjects if it's been tested only on other species.

▶ **Tip 4.** Be cautious with products available exclusively through mail order or the Internet. Why aren't these products for sale in retail health stores? Sometimes the reason is that the product is illegal. There have been reports that some so-called natural pro-hormone supplements are "contaminated" with illegal anabolic drugs. If this is the case, you're not only risking your health by ordering these products but also breaking the law.

▶ **Tip 5.** If in doubt, give the product a tryout. Do your own research study. Buy a small container of the product and take it as directed on the label. Continue your current exercise routine and nutrition program; the only change you have made is adding the trial product. After a month or so, assess whether the product did what it was supposed to. Did you get stronger? Did you gain muscle? Did you lose body fat? Did you suffer side effects? If you didn't get the results you were expecting from the product, it probably doesn't work for you.

chapter 11

HYBRID HARD BODY PROGRAM

In part I of this book, we fired up the power tools for maximizing muscle mass. In part II, we ripped open the complete package for fat loss. So far in part III, we've unveiled the trade secrets of advanced bodybuilding. Now we'll combine all this knowledge and transform your physique to its maximum potential.

If you're looking to forge the ultimate physique, this plan is for you. The hybrid hard body workout combines 30 of the most effective muscle-shaping exercises into a four-day split-training routine. I have included a couple of cardio sessions in the weekly schedule to tease off that fat layer to showcase your hard-earned muscle. The hard body diet provides enough nutrients to fuel muscle growth, while careful calorie control starves your fat stores.

The hybrid system is a blend of techniques, a combination of bodybuilding styles that simultaneously stimulates muscle growth and promotes fat loss. In effect, with the hybrid system you get the best elements of the mass generator program (chapter 4) and the body fat blitz program (chapter 7) and then some.

PROGRAM OVERVIEW

Workout Plan

The hybrid hard body program is an advanced high-intensity body sculpting system designed for simultaneous muscle gain and fat loss. This program is best suited for the advanced bodybuilder. For those of you with less gym experience, I recommend that you spend a few months developing the basic techniques outlined in the previous two programs. If your primary need is muscle mass, use the mass generator program (chapter 4) to build a solid foundation of muscle before moving on to the hybrid hard body program. If your primary need is fat loss, use the body fat blitz program (chapter 7) before you progress to developing your body further.

The hybrid hard body program emphasizes high-intensity training. Perform three sets of each exercise, using weights equivalent to 65 to 75 percent of your one-rep maximum. After an initial warm-up set of 12 reps, increase the weight on the second set so that your muscles fatigue after 10 reps. For the final work set, add more weight and squeeze out 8 reps to failure. To make your muscles work hard, keep your rest intervals short—take 30 seconds rest between the first two sets, 45 seconds between the next two sets, and 60 seconds before the final heavy set.

To gain the maximum benefit from this program, incorporate the high-intensity techniques in chapter 8. Most of the machine-based exercises in this program make it easy to train beyond failure using drop sets, forced reps, and negative reps. Still take the necessary safety precautions and use a spotter.

Here's how the hybrid hard body four-way split-training system works. Session 1 involves the chest, triceps, and abdominals. Session 2 works the back, biceps, and forearms. Session 3 targets the quads, hamstrings, and calves. Session 4 works the shoulders, trapezius, and abs. This sequence groups body parts that share similar exercise biomechanics. For example, in session 1 the *push* exercises for the chest also recruit and warm up the triceps. Similarly, in session 2, the *pull* exercises for the back muscles recruit and warm up the biceps and forearm muscles. In both sessions, the smaller muscle is already pumped and ready for action when its turn comes. The leg muscles have session 3 all to themselves; being the largest muscle group, the quadriceps are hit first in the sequence. The shoulder muscles are trained at the end of the week in session 4, so that the muscles are rested after their assistance work with the pressing exercises in session 1. To achieve complete muscular development, the muscles of the shoulder need their own designated session. You'll be strengthening the muscles of the rotator cuff, shaping all three heads of the deltoid, and building the trapezius muscles. The abdominals, obliques, and serratus muscles are worked in both sessions 1 and 4. I've chosen a sequence of exercises that hit these muscles from all angles, helping you develop a tight midsection and six-pack.

In this program, you exercise each major muscle group once every seven days. Remember that your muscles need five to seven days to fully recover from an intense weights workout. Space your four workout sessions evenly during the week—for example, Monday, Tuesday, Thursday, and Friday. Larger muscles such as the chest, shoulders, back, and quads are each assigned three exercises; and, as a general rule, an isolation exercise is used to prime the muscle before compound movements. Each exercise hits the muscle from a different angle. Targeting different sections of the larger muscles ensures more complete muscular development.

During each 45-minute workout, you push yourself *hard* to achieve your potential. By the third set of each exercise, you should be lifting the heaviest possible weight for eight repetitions to failure, using flawless form. For at least one exercise per body part, you'll train beyond failure, using one or more of the high-intensity techniques in chapter 8.

As you gain experience using this program, feel free to change, add, or subtract exercises to meet your own needs and preferences. The exercises described in all three programs in this book are interchangeable. Just make sure that your exercise combinations hit the larger muscle groups from different angles to ensure proportioned development. Don't add too many extra exercises, or you'll risk overtraining (see chapter 12).

Calorie-burning cardiovascular exercise is also included in this program. If you want that hard body look, you need to keep your body fat low. As I've mentioned, you won't see those rippling muscles or that shredded six-pack unless your body fat is below 10 percent. You should do two 30-minute sessions of continuous, low-resistance cardio on two of the days you're not lifting. Work hard enough to maintain your heart rate in the target zone (70 percent of your maximum heart rate—calculate your target heart rate by subtracting your age from 220 and multiplying by 0.7).

The type of aerobic exercise you do is up to you. Choose from walking, jogging, cycling, stair climbing, jumping rope, or swimming. It's more challenging if you vary the aerobic exercise, selecting a different activity for each cardio session. For example, cycle on a stationary bike during one session, then walk or jog on the treadmill during the other session.

Nutrition Plan

To gain muscle and lose body fat at the same time, consume roughly the same amount of calories that you burn each day. In other words, keep your daily calorie intake close to your maintenance requirement (body weight in pounds multiplied by 10). You want to provide enough calories for muscle growth but force your body to get its additional energy through burning fat stores. The process might need some fine-tuning as you go along. Monitor your progress in terms of muscle gain and fat loss on a weekly basis. If you wish to gain more muscle mass, add 5 percent to your estimated daily calorie requirement; if you need to lose more body fat, subtract 5 percent from your estimated value.

To prevent excess carbohydrates from being stored as fat, the nutrient ratio of your diet should favor protein. Divide your food sources as 50 percent protein, 40 percent carbohydrates, and 10 percent fat.

The 1,800-calorie sample meal plan (table 11.1) is a rough guide for someone who weighs 180 pounds (81.6 kg), based on the estimated daily maintenance value (body weight in pounds multiplied by 10). If you find you need more muscle mass, add 5 percent to this value. So if your body weight is 180 pounds, your maintenance requirement is 180 × 10, or 1,800 calories per day. Since 5 percent of this figure is 90 calories, your daily intake should be 1,800 + 90, or 1,890 calories. On the flip side, if you need to shed more body fat, subtract 5 percent (90 calories) from the maintenance value, which means consuming 1,710 calories per day.

TABLE 11.1

Hybrid Hard Body Sample Meal Plan

Breakfast	Egg white scramble: Mix five egg whites with one tbsp of nonfat milk. Cook in a nonstick pan coated with a nonfat cooking spray. Serve on one piece of whole-wheat toast. Drink one cup of black coffee or water. Calories: 320
Midmorning snack	Meal-replacement drink: Mix one sachet of a meal-replacement powder such as MESO-Tech (MuscleTech) with 12 oz of cold water in a blender. Calories: 340
Lunch	Tuna meal: Microwave one medium-sized potato. Steam a portion of green beans. Serve with one can of water-packed tuna sprinkled with lemon juice. Drink water. Calories: 260
Midafternoon snack	Protein drink: Mix two servings of protein powder such as NITRO-Tech (MuscleTech) with 4 oz water and 4 oz nonfat milk. Add one whole banana. Blend at high speed for 30 seconds. Calories: 300
Dinner	Chicken meal: Prepare a skinless chicken breast by squeezing lemon juice over it. Grill until cooked. Serve with a portion of steamed brown rice and broccoli. 1 tbsp of tomato ketchup is optional. Calories: 380
Late-evening snack	One low-carb protein bar such as NITRO-Tech bar (MuscleTech). Calories: 290
Daily values (approximate)	Protein: 225 g (900 cal), 50% Carbs: 180 g (720 cal), 40% Fat: 20 g (180 cal), 10% Total calories: 1,800

Adjusting the sample meal plan to your weight is easy, based on the fact that one gram of protein is four calories, one gram of carbohydrates is four calories, and one gram of fat is nine calories. Every 10 pounds (4.5 kg) in body weight is equivalent to 100 calories. Keeping the nutrient ratio at 50 percent protein and 40 percent carbohydrates, 100 calories equals 15 grams of protein (60 calories) plus 10 grams of carbohydrates (40 calories). To increase or decrease the calorie content to match your body weight, add or subtract these amounts from the sample meal plan.

Adjust your protein intake by changing the amount of protein powder you add to your midafternoon snack or changing the number of egg whites you eat at breakfast (one egg white contains six grams of protein). Similarly, by adjusting your portions of pasta or rice at lunch and dinner, you can easily increase or decrease your intake of carbohydrates.

Remember that the nutrition values in the sample meal plan (table 11.1) are only approximate. Check nutrition labels on the products you buy because values vary among brands.

As mentioned, the 1,800-calorie sample meal plan is a rough guide for someone who weighs 180 pounds. Adjust the content of the sample meal plan to your body weight, using table 11.2.

TABLE 11.2

Maintenance Daily Calorie Intake Based on Body Weight (Hybrid Hard Body Program)

Body weight (lbs)	Calories per day	Protein	Carbohydrates	Fat
220	2,200	275 g/1,100 cal	220 g/880 cal	24 g/220 cal
200	2,000	250 g/1,000 cal	200 g/800 cal	22 g/200 cal
180	1,800	225 g/900 cal	180 g/720 cal	20 g/180 cal
160	1,600	200 g/800 cal	160 g/640 cal	18 g/160 cal
140	1,400	175 g/700 cal	140 g/560 cal	16 g/140 cal

Nutrient ratio: 50% protein, 40% carbohydrates, 10% fat
Calorie value: 1 g protein = 4 calories; 1 g carbohydrates = 4 calories; 1 g fat = 9 calories
Daily calorie intake = body weight in pounds × 10

Some of the dietary supplements listed in chapter 10 can also aid your progress in the hybrid hard body program. In particular, creatine helps build muscle mass; a fat burner can help tease off unwanted body fat.

Progress Measurements

Monitoring your progress is essential because fine-tuning your workouts and diet is key to advanced bodybuilding. Measure your body weight using a scale and take body measurements—chest, waist, arm, thigh, and calf circumference—with a tape measure. Measure body fat percentage using a skin caliper. Following the manufacturer's instructions, record the skin thickness at three sites on your body, usually the upper arm, waist, and thigh. Calculate the average reading by adding all three measurements then dividing by three. You can also check your progress in the mirror. Check if each muscle group is developing in proportion. Lagging muscle groups might need more attention (see chapter 12). If you want that athletic V-taper, be sure to work your side deltoids and those outer lats and narrow that waist by losing body fat.

Measure muscle strength by recording the maximum weight you can lift for six repetitions during the last set of each exercise. The stronger the muscle becomes, the bigger it grows. The larger your muscle mass, the more fat you'll burn. To continue gaining size and strength, increase the weight on each exercise by 5 percent every two weeks.

Measure fitness during an aerobic exercise of your choice, such as cycling or jogging. Monitor how long you can sustain your heart rate at 70 percent of its maximum value. A person of average fitness should be able to sustain 70 percent maximum heart rate for 20 minutes (maximum heart rate equals 220 minus age in years multiplied by 0.7). Each week, aim to increase your cardio time by 10 minutes or increase your target heart rate by 5 percent. The harder you work for 30 minutes, the more calories you'll burn. The more calories you use, the more fat you lose.

Results

After six weeks on this program, you should gain three to four pounds of muscle and lose three pounds of body fat. You'll add an inch to your chest, lose an inch from your waist, and boost your arm and thigh circumference by half an inch. As a result of this simultaneous muscle gain and fat loss, you should experience a 10 percent increase in strength and a 3 percent drop in body fat. Because you'll be gaining muscle and losing fat simultaneously, your body weight might not change much within six weeks on this program. Don't be alarmed—your gain in muscular weight is being offset by the loss of body fat. Your body measurements and body fat percentage are better indicators of your progress than are changes in your body weight.

HYBRID HARD BODY WORKOUT

Hybrid Hard Body Exercise Program

Routine: Four-way split
Cycle: Four days per week weight training, two days cardio
Schedule: Monday, Tuesday, Thursday, Friday, plus two sessions for cardio
Goal: Muscle gain and fat loss
Detail: 3 sets of 12, 10, 8 reps
Rest interval: 30 to 60 seconds
Workout time: 45 minutes

CHEST, TRICEPS, AND ABS MONDAY	
Chest	Machine chest flys
	Machine incline presses
	Decline bench presses
Triceps	Tricep dips
	One-arm triceps pushdowns
Abs	Rope crunches
	Cable side crunches
BACK, BICEPS, AND FOREARMS TUESDAY	
Back	Reverse-grip pulldowns
	Dumbbell rows
	Lumbar extensions
Biceps	Preacher curls
	Concentration curls
Forearms	Barbell wrist curls
	Reverse wrist curls
CARDIO WEDNESDAY	
Cardio	Cycling (30 minutes)

LEGS THURSDAY	
Quadriceps	Leg extensions
	Leg presses
	Hack squats
Hamstrings	Leg curls
	Straight-leg deadlifts
Calves	Seated calf raises
	Straight-leg calf raises
SHOULDERS AND ABS FRIDAY	
Rotator cuff	External rotations
	Internal rotations
	Cable lateral raises
Shoulders	Machine lateral raises
	Rear deltoid flys
	Front deltoid raises
Trapezius	Shrugs
Abs	Machine crunches
	Bench leg raises
CARDIO SATURDAY	
Cardio	Treadmill (30 minutes) walking or jogging

CHEST, TRICEPS, AND ABS (MONDAY)
Chest

MACHINE CHEST FLYS

This is a variation of the dumbbell chest fly (see page 41) but done using a machine with either a hand grip or elbow pads. The chest fly machine is better suited to techniques of high intensity. Sit on the fly machine with the seat positioned so that the handles are at shoulder level (figure 11.1a). Grab the handles and squeeze them together until they're touching in front of you (figure 11.1b).

Pause momentarily to contract your pecs forcibly before resisting back to the full stretch. Don't allow your hands to pass behind the plane of your body. Keep your elbows nearly straight just below shoulder level at all times.

▶ **CHECK IT!** If your upper pecs are small relative to the rest of your chest, substitute this exercise with incline dumbbell flys. If your lower pecs need more attention, perform cable crossovers instead.

Figure 11.1 Machine chest flys: *(a)* sit at the machine; *(b)* squeeze handles in front of chest.

Chest *(continued)*

MACHINE INCLINE PRESSES

Place an adjustable exercise bench beneath the bar of a Smith machine; tilt the backrest head-up at an angle of 30 to 45 degrees. Before you load the machine with weight, lie back on the bench and check the trajectory of the bar. Position the bench so that the bar touches the midpoint of your chest when lowered. Position your feet firmly on the floor. Take an overhand grip on the barbell, palms turned forward, hands slightly wider than shoulder-width apart. Release the bar from the uprights; hold the bar above your chest with arms extended (figure 11.2a). Begin the repetition by bending your elbows.

> ▶ **CHECK IT!** Hold the bar just short of full lockout on the way up to keep the tension on the chest muscles.

Lower the weight slowly to the midpoint of your chest, just above the nipple line (figure 11.2b). Inhale as you lower the weight. Let the bar touch your chest and hold for one second. Then push the weight vertically upward to the starting position. Hold the bar momentarily contracting your pecs, then repeat.

You can perform this exercise using a barbell (chapter 4), a pair of dumbbells (chapter 7), or on any incline press machine.

Figure 11.2 Machine incline presses: *(a)* **hold the bar above your chest;** *(b)* **lower the bar.**

141

Chest *(continued)*

DECLINE BENCH PRESSES

Position an adjustable decline bench at an angle of 25 to 30 degrees in relation to the ground. Lie supine on the bench with a dumbbell in each hand. Hook your feet under the ankle pads. Press the dumbbells up until your elbows are fully extended over your chest, palms turned forward (figure 11.3a). From the start position, lower the dumbbells vertically downward by bending your elbows down and back. Keep the dumbbells in line, with your palms turned forward. The weights should travel perpendicular to the floor. Lower the dumbbells until they are beside your chest at nipple level (figure 11.3b). Press the weights vertically upward back to the start position. Squeeze the pec muscles as the dumbbells touch in the lockout position. Hold one second and repeat.

You can also do this exercise using the bar on the Smith machine.

Figure 11.3 Decline bench presses: *(a)* hold the dumbbells over your chest; *(b)* lower the dumbbells to your chest.

Triceps

TRICEPS DIPS

Grab the parallel bars and lift yourself up until your arms are fully extended (figure 11.4a). Let your thighs hang downward; bend your knees slightly and hook one foot over the other. From this start position, bend your elbows and slowly lower your body until your upper arms are parallel to the floor (figure 11.4b). Keep your torso upright and your elbows close to your sides. Pause momentarily in the bottom position, then push yourself back up until your elbows lock out. Contract your triceps forcibly at the top for a one count, then repeat.

If dips on the parallel bars are too difficult or too easy, perform the exercise seated in the triceps pushdown machine. Grab the handles with your palms turned in. In the start position, your elbows should bend to 90 degrees with upper arms parallel to the floor. Push the weight down until your arms are fully straight and your elbows lock out. Contract your triceps momentarily, then slowly return the weight to the start position and repeat.

Figure 11.4 Triceps dips: *(a)* support yourself on the bars; *(b)* lower your torso down.

Triceps *(continued)*

ONE-ARM TRICEPS PUSHDOWNS

Attach a D-handle to the cable of a high pulley machine. Grab the handle in one hand with an underhand grip, palm facing upward. Position your upper arm perpendicular in relation to the floor, with your elbow fully bent (figure 11.5a). From the start position, straighten your arm, pushing the handle down. Keep your upper arm fixed during this exercise, restricting motion exclusively to your elbow. Hold the lockout position momentarily, contracting your triceps muscle

(figure 11.5b). Then slowly return the handle to the start position and repeat. After you've completed the set number of reps with one arm, do the same with your opposite arm.

Figure 11.5 One-arm triceps pushdowns: *(a)* hold the handle with your elbow bent; *(b)* push down toward the floor.

Abs

ROPE CRUNCHES

Connect a rope attachment to the cable of a high pulley and kneel on the floor beneath it, holding the ends of the rope in your hands. Pull the rope down and hold it behind your head (figure 11.6a). From this position, contract your abdominals to curl your torso down (figure 11.6b). Restrict movement exclusively to bending your spine. Your elbows should come down and back toward your knees, but the position of your hands and shoulders should not change. Hold momentarily to contract your abdominals on completion of the crunch, then slowly return to the start position and repeat.

If you don't have access to a cable pulley machine, do decline sit-ups (chapter 4) as a substitute.

Figure 11.6 Rope crunches: *(a)* **hold the rope behind your head;** *(b)* **curl your torso.**

Abs (continued)

CABLE SIDE CRUNCHES

Attach a D-handle to the high pulley of a cable machine. Grab the handle with one hand and kneel on the floor beneath the pulley. Hold the handle close to the side of your head with your elbow bent (figure 11.7a). Crunch downward, directing your elbow to the opposite knee (figure 11.7b). Restrict movement exclusively to bending your spine. The angle of your arm at the shoulder should not change. Hold the

> ▸ **CHECK IT!** During this exercise, feel the oblique muscles contracting with your free hand.

side crunch position momentarily, squeezing your oblique muscles—feel them contract with your free hand. Then slowly return to the start position and repeat. After completing the set number of reps, switch hands and work the opposite side. You can also do this exercise in a standing position.

If you don't have access to a cable pulley, do twisting sit-ups (chapter 7) as a substitute to work the serratus and oblique muscles.

Figure 11.7 Cable side crunches: (a) hold the handle adjacent to your head; (b) crunch down toward the opposite knee.

BACK, BICEPS, AND FOREARMS (TUESDAY)
Back

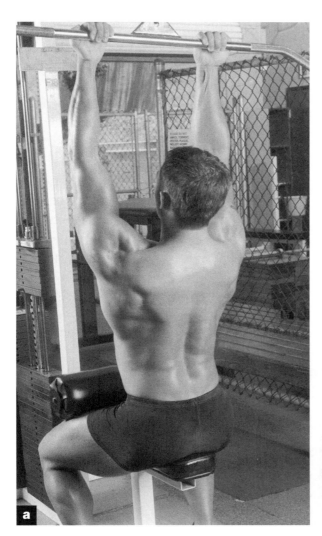

REVERSE-GRIP PULLDOWNS

Sit at a cable pulldown machine facing inward; position your thighs under the knee pads. Grasp the bar with a reverse underhand grip, palms turned toward you. Position your hands about shoulder-width apart. With your arms fully extended overhead, lean your torso back about 30 degrees from the vertical plane (figure 11.8a). Begin the repetition by pulling the bar down to the top of your chest (figure 11.8b). Think of your hands as hooks. Make your upper back muscles do the work, pulling your elbows down and back. Hold the bar above your collar bone for one second, contracting the latissimus muscles. Then slowly return the weight to the start position.

If you don't have access to a pulldown machine, you can do the same movement using a chin-up bar.

> ► **CHECK IT!** Don't pull the bar below collar bone level. Don't lean back too far or pull the weight down with momentum.

Figure 11.8 Reverse-grip pulldowns: *(a)* take an underhand grip on the bar; *(b)* pull the bar to your chest.

Back *(continued)*

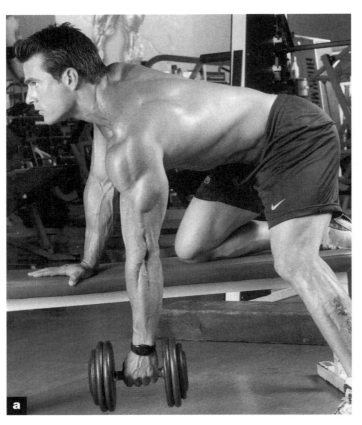

DUMBBELL ROWS

Stand alongside a flat exercise bench. Rest one knee on the bench and lean forward, supporting your torso with the arm nearest the bench. Your back should be straight and just above parallel to the floor. Reach down and pick up a dumbbell with your free hand. Hold the weight with your arm extended vertically downward so that the dumbbell is parallel to the bench (figure 11.9a). From the start position, bend the elbow and pull the weight vertically upward until the dumbbell is level with your torso. Pause for a second at the top, contracting your upper back muscles

> ▶ **CHECK IT!** Look straight ahead in order to keep your back straight. Pull your elbow up as high as possible without twisting your torso. Avoid jerking the weight upward.

(figure 11.9b). Then slowly lower the weight down to the start position without touching the ground. Repeat. Keep your forearm hanging straight down throughout the movement. After you complete the planned number of reps, switch position and continue the set using the opposite arm.

You can do the row exercise using a barbell (chapter 4) or in a seated position using a low pulley cable (chapter 7). My personal favorite is the seated row machine, with a built-in chest pad that reduces the strain on the lower back. Performing the row exercise using one arm at a time affords a more satisfying squeeze in the latissimus muscle.

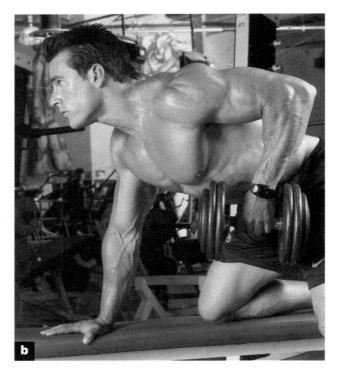

Figure 11.9 Dumbbell rows: *(a)* grip the dumbbell in one hand; *(b)* lift the weight straight upward.

Back *(continued)*

LUMBAR EXTENSIONS

Position yourself face down across the lumbar extension apparatus with your hips supported on the bench and your heels secured under the ankle pads. Bend forward at the waist so that your torso hangs down toward the floor. Cross your arms in front of your chest (figure 11.10a). In the start position, your torso should be perpendicular at 90 degrees to your thighs. Begin the exercise by lifting your body at the waist (figure 11.10b). Straighten all the way up until your torso is slightly above parallel to the ground. The angle of your spine should change from being curled forward to arched slightly backward at full extension. Despite the name of this exercise, do not hyperextend your lower back because this places excess pressure on the joints of your spine. Momentarily hold the extended position just above parallel before slowly returning to the start position.

> ▸ **CHECK IT!** To make the lower back muscles work harder, hold a weight plate across the front of your chest.

You can make this exercise less strenuous by using an incline extension bench. The ankle support is lower to the ground, and your legs make a 45-degree angle to the floor.

Figure 11.10   Lumbar extensions: *(a)* **lie over an extension bench;** *(b)* **lift your torso to just beyond parallel.**

Biceps

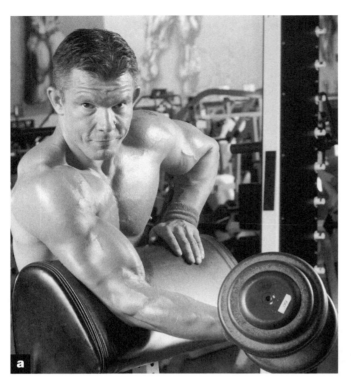

PREACHER CURLS

Sit facing a preacher bench with the pad touching your lower chest. The pad should slope away from the front of your body at about 45 degrees. Grab a dumbbell in one hand and rest the back of your upper arm on the pad. The pad should support your arm from the armpit to the elbow. In the starting position, your arm is out straight with your palm turned up (figure 11.11.a). Begin the repetition by bending your elbow, curling the dumbbell up until it reaches shoulder level (figure 11.11b). Pause at the top for a second, contracting the biceps. Slowly lower the weight. Stop 10 degrees short of full elbow extension to keep tension on the biceps at the bottom of the lift. Hold the weight for one second and repeat. The preacher bench isolates the biceps muscle because movement can occur only at the elbow. At the completion of the set, switch hands and perform the same movement with the other arm.

Perform preacher curls using a barbell or a biceps curl machine with a sloping arm rest.

Figure 11.11 Preacher curls: *(a)* **rest arm on preacher bench with dumbbell in hand;** *(b)* **curl dumbbell to shoulder.**

Biceps *(continued)*

CONCENTRATION CURLS

Grab a dumbbell and sit on the edge of a flat bench. Rest the back of your upper arm against the inside of your thigh. In the start position, your arm is straight and your palm turned up (figure 11.12a). Lift the dumbbell toward your shoulder (figure 11.12b). Keep your upper arm and torso still; let your biceps do the work. When the dumbbell reaches shoulder level, pause for one second, then slowly lower the weight. Stop a few degrees short of full extension to keep tension on your biceps. Pause momentarily and repeat. When you have completed the set, switch the dumbbell to your other hand to work the opposite biceps.

You can also do this exercise using a D-handle attached to the cable of a low pulley.

Figure 11.12 Concentration curls: *(a)* **sit on a flat bench with a dumbbell in one hand;** *(b)* **curl the dumbbell toward your shoulder.**

Forearms

a

BARBELL WRIST CURLS

Sit on a flat exercise bench. Grab a barbell in a shoulder-width underhand grip, palms turned up. Position the back of your forearms on the tops of your thighs so that your wrists hang over your knees (figure 11.13a). Or you can rest your forearms on the bench between your thighs. Lower the weight slowly by bending your wrists toward the floor (figure 11.13b). Feel the muscles of your forearm stretch and hold in the bottom position momentarily. Curl the weight up using wrist motion. Your elbows should not move, and the backs of your forearms should remain in contact

b

with your thighs. Hold the contracted position for one second, then slowly lower the weight to the start position and repeat.

> ▶ **CHECK IT!** In the ideal position for this exercise, your forearms make a 45-degree angle to the floor. Try resting your forearms on a preacher bench and see if this works better for you.

Figure 11.13 Barbell wrist curls: *(a)* **hold the barbell so that your wrists hang over your knees;** *(b)* **lower the weight by bending your wrists.**

Forearms *(continued)*

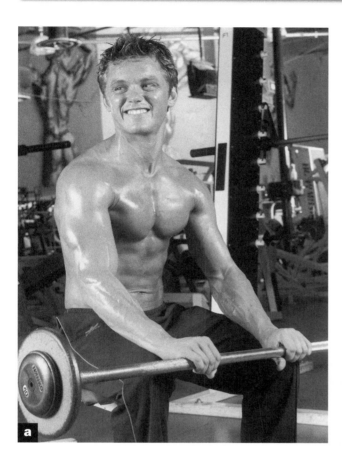

REVERSE WRIST CURLS

As the name suggests, the reverse wrist curl is identical to the standard wrist curl except you take a reverse overhand grip on the bar, palms turned down. This exercise works the muscles on the backside of your forearm. The fronts of your forearms rest on your thighs or the bench so that your hands are hanging off the edge (figure 11.14a). Slowly lower the weight by bending your wrists toward the floor (figure 11.14b). Feel the muscles stretch; hold for one count. Curl the weight up, moving the back of your hands toward you. Motion should occur at the wrist, not the elbow. Your forearms remain in contact with your thighs or the bench.

Hold the contracted position for one second, then slowly lower the weight and repeat.

You can do this exercise using a preacher bench or with a dumbbell in each hand in place of the barbell.

Figure 11.14 Reverse wrist curls: *(a)* **hold the barbell so your wrists hang over your knees;** *(b)* **lower the weight by bending your wrists.**

CARDIO (WEDNESDAY)

Perform 30 minutes of aerobic exercise. Choose from cycling, walking, jogging, stair climbing, or jumping rope.

LEGS (THURSDAY)
Quadriceps

LEG EXTENSIONS

Sit at a leg extension machine. Adjust the backrest so that the backs of your knees fit snugly against the seat and your thighs are supported. Position your ankles under the roller pad. If the pad is adjustable, position it so it rests just above your ankles on the lowest part of your shins. Grip the handles on the sides of the machine for support (figure 11.15a). From the starting position, contract your quadriceps to straighten your knees (figure 11.15b). Lift the weight all the way up until your knees are straight. Pause for one second at the top and flex your quadri-

ceps. Slowly lower the weight until your knees are bent to 90 degrees. Hold the weight momentarily in the bottom position and repeat.

▶ **CHECK IT!** Don't let your hips rise off the seat.

Figure 11.15 Leg extensions: *(a)* get into position in a leg extension machine; *(b)* straighten your legs.

Quadriceps *(continued)*

LEG PRESSES

Get into position on the seat of a leg press machine. Place your feet about shoulder-width apart on the foot plate, toes pointing out slightly. In the start position, your legs should be fully straight with knees locked (figure 11.16a). Before you begin, use the handle to release the weight support. Slowly lower the weight until your knees bend to 90 degrees (figure 11.16b).

At this point, your thighs should lightly touch your abdomen. Inhale deeply as the weight is lowered. Push the weight back to the start position by straightening your knees. Exhale as you lift the weight. If you want to keep tension on the quadriceps, don't quite lock out your knees at the top.

▸ **CHECK IT!** The backrest should be at a 45- to 60-degree angle to the seat. When the angle is closer to 90 degrees, excessive strain is placed on your lower spine.

Figure 11.16 Leg presses: *(a)* **sit in a leg press machine with legs straight;** *(b)* **lower the weight by bending your knees.**

Quadriceps *(continued)*

HACK SQUATS

Place your shoulders under the pads of the hack-squat machine with your spine against the backrest. Stand with your feet shoulder-width apart on the foot plate, toes pointing forward (figure 11.17a). This is the start position. Begin the repetition by bending your knees and slowly lowering your hips straight down until your knees make an angle of 90 degrees (figure 11.17b). During the movement, keep your back against the pad, your chin up, and your head looking

▶ **CHECK IT!** To reduce the chance of knee injury, avoid squatting too deeply. Position your feet about six inches in front of the plane of your body during hack squats.

forward. Once you reach the bottom position, push the weight up using your thighs and hips until your knees are straight. On the hack-squat machine, the plane of motion is inclined at about 60 degrees to the ground. Inhale deeply during the descent and exhale on the way up.

If you don't have access to a hack-squat machine, you can use a Smith machine (chapter 7) or do standard barbell squats, as described on page 48 in chapter 4.

Figure 11.17 Hack squats: *(a)* get into position in the machine; *(b)* lower the weight by bending your knees.

Hamstrings

LEG CURLS

Lie facedown on a leg curl machine and position the backs of your ankles under the roller pads (figure 11.18a). Grip the handles for support. From the start position, curl the weight up by bending your knees (figure 11.18b). Try to bring your heels to your buttocks. When the roller pad touches the backs of your hamstrings, hold the contracted position for one second. Slowly return the weight to the start position until your legs are

▶ **CHECK IT!** Don't lift your hips off the machine.

almost straight. Hold at the bottom momentarily and then repeat.

You can also do this exercise using a standing leg curl machine working one leg at a time, as described in chapter 7.

Figure 11.18 Leg curls: *(a)* **get into position on the leg curl machine;** *(b)* **curl the weight toward your buttocks.**

Hamstrings (continued)

STRAIGHT-LEG DEADLIFTS

Pick up a barbell in an overhand grip (palms down) with your hands shoulder-width apart. Stand straight, holding the barbell at arms' length in front of you. Place your feet directly below your hips, toes pointing forward (figure 11.19a). From the start position, bend forward at the hips, slowly lowering the barbell vertically downward (figure 11.19b). Don't bend at the knees. Keep your back straight and your chin up. Descend until the weight passes below knee level and you feel your hamstring

> ► **CHECK IT!** Don't hunch your back. If your hamstrings are tight, you can allow a slight bend at your knees, but no more than 20 degrees.

muscles stretch. Don't allow the weight to touch the floor. At the bottom, contract your hamstrings and gluteus muscles to lift the weight back to the start position.

Figure 11.19 Straight-leg deadlifts: *(a)* hold the barbell at arms' length; *(b)* lower the weight, keeping your knees locked.

Calves

SEATED CALF RAISES

Position yourself on a seated calf machine. Place the balls of your feet on the platform and the knee pad on the front of your lower thighs. Your knees should be in line with your hips with your toes directly below your knees (figure 11.20a). Release the safety catch and grip the handles. Slowly lower your heels as far as you can, stretching your calf muscles but keeping your toes firmly on the platform (figure 11.20b). In the bottom position, hold the stretch for one second. Contract your calf muscles and push the weight as high as possible, as if you were standing on tiptoes. Flex hard at the top and hold for another one count. Slowly lower the weight and repeat.

▶ **CHECK IT!** Don't rest the pad too high on your thighs. It should be placed just above your knees.

Figure 11.20 Seated calf raises: (a) **sit in a seated calf machine;** (b) **lower your heels.**

Calves *(continued)*

STRAIGHT-LEG CALF RAISES

Get into position on the seat of a leg press machine. Place the balls of both feet on the lower edge of the foot plate, about six inches apart, toes pointing forward. Make sure that your heels are free to move beneath the foot plate. Lock your knees out straight so that motion occurs exclusively at the ankles. From the start position (figure 11.21a), push the weight up as far as you can. Hold the "tip-toe" position momentarily and contract your calf muscles (figure 11.21b). Then slowly lower the weight back to the start position. In the bottom position, pause to stretch the calf muscles, then repeat.

▸ **CHECK IT!** Keep your knees stiff throughout the movement.

Several machines are designed for you to perform straight-leg calf raises in a seated position with a support for the lumbar spine. If you don't have access to a leg press or calf sled machine, perform standing calf raises (chapter 4) or donkey calf raises (chapter 7).

Figure 11.21 Straight-leg calf raises: *(a)* **position your feet on the foot plate;** *(b)* **push the weight upward, pointing your toes.**

SHOULDERS AND ABS (FRIDAY)
Rotator Cuff

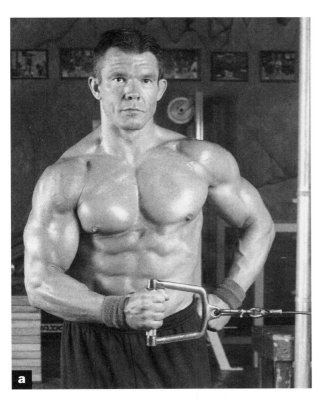

EXTERNAL ROTATIONS

External rotations build the infraspinatus and teres minor muscles that lie behind the shoulder under the rear deltoid. Adjust the cable pulley to waist height. Stand with the left side of your body beside the weight stack. Grab the cable handle with your right hand, palm turned toward the pulley. Position your right elbow firmly against your waist, elbow bent at 90 degrees and forearm parallel to the floor (figure 11.22a). Begin with the handle at the midline of your body and move your hand toward your right side as far as it will go (figure 11.22b). Be sure to stand far enough away from the pulley so that the cable remains under tension. Keep your elbow fixed at your side and your forearm parallel to the floor throughout the movement. Your hand should move through an arc of approximately 90 degrees. Hold the contracted position momentarily before slowly returning to the start position. After completing the set, switch position and perform with the left hand.

▶ **CHECK IT!** Only the hand and forearm move during this exercise. Keep the elbow and upper arm tight against the side of your body. The motion resembles the hand of a clock moving back and forth between 10 o'clock and 2 o'clock.

You can also do this exercise by tying one end of a rubber exercise band around a fixed upright support at waist height.

Figure 11.22 External rotations: (a) start with the handle at the middle of your body; (b) pull handle outward to the right.

Rotator Cuff *(continued)*

INTERNAL ROTATIONS

Internal rotations build the subscapularis muscle that lies under the front deltoid. Adjust the cable pulley to waist height. Stand with the left side of your body beside the weight stack. Grab the cable handle with your left hand, palm turned away from the pulley. Position your left elbow firmly against your waist, elbow bent at 90 degrees and forearm parallel to the floor (figure 11.23a). With the handle out to the side, pull the cable inward across the front of your

body (figure 11.23b). Keep your elbow fixed at your side and your forearm parallel to the floor at all times. Hold the contracted position momentarily, then return slowly to the start position. Be sure to stand far enough away from the pulley so that the cable remains under tension throughout. Your hand should move through an arc of about 90 to 120 degrees. When the set is complete, switch position and perform with the right hand.

> ▸ **CHECK IT!** Only the hand and forearm move during this exercise. Keep your elbow and upper arm tight against the side of your body. The motion resembles the hand of a clock moving between 10 o'clock and 2 o'clock.

You can also do this exercise by tying one end of a rubber exercise band at waist height around an upright support.

Figure 11.23 Internal rotations: *(a)* grab the handle out to your side; *(b)* pull the handle across your body.

Rotator Cuff *(continued)*

CABLE LATERAL RAISES (ABDUCTION)

This exercise strengthens the supraspinatus muscle, which lies over the top of the shoulder. The movement is similar to the dumbbell lateral raise for the deltoid (chapter 4, page 43). Position the cable pulley at floor level. Stand with your left side next to the weight stack. Grasp the handle attached to the low pulley with your right hand crossed over your body (figure 11.24a). Raise your hand up and out in a wide arc (figure 11.24b). Keep your hand slightly in front of the plane of your body. Keep your elbow fairly straight; it should not move during the movement. Raise your hand to shoulder level, hold momentarily, then slowly lower the weight to the start position. After completing the set, switch position and face the other direction. Repeat the exercise with your left hand.

> ► **CHECK IT!** The supraspinatus muscle is worked best during the first 60 degrees of this motion, so there's no need to raise your hand above shoulder level.

Figure 11.24 Cable lateral raises: *(a)* grab the handle on the low pulley; *(b)* raise your hand in a wide arc.

Shoulders

MACHINE LATERAL RAISES

Position yourself in the seated deltoid raise machine with your spine upright. Adjust the seat height so that your elbows align with the pads. Your upper arms should be positioned vertical by your sides. If the machine has handles, grasp them with both hands. From the start position (figure 11.25a), raise your elbows outward and upward from the side of your body (figure 11.25b), until your upper arms are parallel to the floor. Pause momentarily when your elbows reach shoulder level and contract the deltoid muscles forcibly. Then slowly lower your elbows back to the start position and repeat.

▶ **CHECK IT!** Don't raise your elbows too high because this places unwanted stress on the shoulder joints.

If you don't have access to a deltoid raise machine, do this exercise using dumbbells, as described in chapters 4 and 7.

Figure 11.25 Machine lateral raises: *(a)* position elbows against pads; *(b)* raise elbows upward.

Shoulders *(continued)*

REAR DELTOID FLYS

Sit facing the deltoid fly machine with your chest against the pad. Adjust the seat height so your arms are parallel to the floor when you grasp the handles. From the starting position (figure 11.26a), slowly pull the handles back until your arms make a straight line across your body. Hold for one second, contracting the rear deltoid muscle (figure 11.26b). Slowly return to the starting position and repeat. Keep your elbows slightly bent with arms parallel to the floor throughout the movement. This exercise works the rear portion of the deltoid muscle, which overlies the back of the shoulder.

If you do not have access to a rear deltoid machine or reverse chest fly machine, this exercise can be performed using dumbbells with your torso bent forward at the waist.

Figure 11.26 Rear deltoid flys: *(a)* sit facing the machine and grasp the handles; *(b)* pull your hands back in an arc.

Shoulders *(continued)*

FRONT DELTOID RAISES

Grab a dumbbell by interlocking the fingers of both hands around the bar. Let your arms hang straight down in front of you. Hold the dumbbell vertically with the uppermost weight resting against your thumbs (figure 11.27a). From this start position, perform a front raise by lifting the dumbbell up in front of you. Motion occurs exclusively at the shoulder; keep your elbows nearly straight. Stop the raise when the dumbbell reaches eye level and your arms are parallel to the floor (figure 11.27b). Hold this position momentarily, squeezing a contraction in your front deltoids. Lower the weight slowly down to the start position, then repeat.

> ▸ **CHECK IT!** Holding the dumbbell is easier if you rest the inside of the upper end against your interlocked thumbs and index fingers.

You can also do this exercise with a dumbbell in each hand. Raise one dumbbell at a time, working the right and left deltoids alternately.

Figure 11.27 Front deltoid raises: *(a)* hold the dumbbell at arms' length; *(b)* raise the dumbbell forward.

Trapezius

SHRUGS

Shrugs build the trapezius muscles in the space between your neck and shoulder. The traps also pass down behind your neck, forming the central portion of your upper back. To perform shrugs, stand upright with a dumbbell in each hand, hands hanging at your sides (figure 11.28a). With your palms turned in, shrug your shoulders as high as you can (figure 11.28b). Try to touch your ears with the tops of both shoulders. Hold the contracted position for one second. Slowly lower the weights, stretching your traps in the bottom position. Hold for one count and repeat. Restrict motion to your shoulder girdle; don't bend your elbows. Look straight ahead and keep your back erect. Move the weight vertically up and down about six inches.

You can also do this exercise using a barbell held at arms' length in front with palms turned toward you. Personally, I prefer machine shrugs.

Figure 11.28 Shrugs: *(a)* **stand with dumbbells in hand;** *(b)* **bring your shoulders toward your ears.**

Abdominals

MACHINE CRUNCHES

Sit on the seat of an abdominal crunch machine. Grasp the handles beside you or place your elbows on the pads. Place your feet on the floor or secure them under the ankle pads, if there are any. From the start position (figure 11.29a), crunch down with your abdominal muscles, curling your torso toward your knees. Hold momentarily in the crunch position, forcibly contracting your abs (figure 11.29b). Then slowly return to the start position and repeat.

If your don't have access to an abdominal crunch machine, do floor crunches (chapter 7) or decline sit-ups (chapter 4) to work your upper abdominal muscles.

Figure 11.29 Machine crunches: *(a)* sit in the seat of the ab machine; *(b)* crunch your torso downward.

Abdominals (continued)

BENCH LEG RAISES

Sit on the edge of a flat exercise bench. Grip the bench behind you. With knees slightly bent, allow your legs to hang down, heels almost touching the floor. Lean back until your torso makes a 45-degree angle to the bench. Support yourself with your hands (figure 11.30a). Begin the exercise by pulling your thighs toward your chest, keeping your legs together (figure 11.30b). Tighten your lower abdominals as your hips bend up. Stop before your thighs become vertical and hold the contracted position for one

second. Slowly lower your legs. Stop before your heels make contact with the ground. Hold in the bottom position for one count and repeat. This is a terrific exercise for the lower abdominals.

Figure 11.30 Bench leg raises: *(a)* **sit on the bench;** *(b)* **pull your thighs to your chest.**

CARDIO (SATURDAY)

Perform 30 minutes of aerobic exercise. Choose from cycling, walking, jogging, stair climbing, or jumping rope.

MUSCLE CARE AND MAINTENANCE

Does the clang of iron plates get your adrenaline pumping? I bet you love a fierce challenge at the bench press or the squat rack. Am I right? First, two 45-pound (20.4-kg) plates on the bar, then four, then even more, gradually building up to your personal best weight. Sweating under that barbell during the final few reps becomes a life-or-death situation, with only one winner. It's either you or the weight.

It's a great sense of achievement to beat that heavy barbell. And we all know that a powerful body is eye candy to casual onlookers. But there's one problem. All that heavy duty pushes your body to the limit. At the end of the day, there's always a bigger weight that's capable of demolishing your joints, tearing your tendons, or ripping your muscle in two.

No one is injury resistant, and no body is indestructible. Even Superman has a weakness. It doesn't matter how big or strong you are, there's always kryptonite lurking somewhere in the gym. So here's the thing: Never underestimate your potential for injury. The phrase "no pain, no gain" might be highlighted in the bodybuilder's bible, but it's not one of the 10 commandments of injury prevention.

MUSCLE CARE

Of all the potential pitfalls that prevent bodybuilding progress, injury throws the biggest wrench in the works. Because of this, the painful pitfall of injury deserves special attention. Most injuries can be prevented or treated if you take the right steps. One step not to take is to neglect or ignore the problem.

Like any other machine, your body demands care and attention. If you abuse the machine or neglect its upkeep, it won't function to the best of its ability. So let's talk about exercising safely. As the saying goes, an ounce of prevention is better than a pound of cure.

Causes of Injury

Several factors play roles in weight-training injury. The most common causes of injury include

▶ technical error,
▶ lifting too much weight,
▶ overtraining,
▶ poor equipment, and
▶ inexperience.

Technical error occurs when you're doing something wrong, when you perform an exercise with incorrect form (for example, using inappropriate hand or foot spacing, arching your back, or swinging the weights). Forgetting to warm up before a workout also counts as a technical error. The technical tips that accompany the exercises in this book will help you maintain correct form.

Using a weight that's too heavy is a common mistake that leads to injury. Always choose a weight that allows you to perform at least four to six repetitions before failure. Make sure you have a spotter if you're under a barbell.

Too much exercise, or overtraining, is another common cause of injury. This situation arises when you train too long and your muscles become overfatigued. Or when you're exercising too often and not allowing your body enough time to recover. The overfatigued or underrecovered muscle is a sitting duck for injury. To avoid overtraining, keep your workouts under an hour and allow adequate rest in your workout schedule.

The type and location of weight-training equipment you choose also affect your chance of injury—in particular, whether you choose to train at home and whether you use free weights or machines. Surveys show that most weight-training injuries (40 percent) occur at home. Apparently, poor equipment and

MUSCLE CARE AND MAINTENANCE **173**

lack of supervision (no spotter) are to blame. When comparing machines and free weights, machines are safer. Two of three weight-training injuries involve using free weights. This probably comes as no surprise. I bet most of you veteran lifters can recall getting trapped under a barbell bench press or dropping a heavy dumbbell on your foot. If your goal is to be safety conscious, I recommend that you join a good gym and strap yourself into their machines.

Injury rates are high among novices. It takes time and practice to master lifting techniques. However, inexperience does not plague just the newcomers to the gym. Whenever you try a new exercise, you become a novice for a while. You might have years of gym experience under your lifting belt, but if you've never done a deadlift, you've got to learn the technique. If you don't respect the exercise during your first few sessions, you could end up with a nasty back injury. There's no substitute for the careful practice of new exercise techniques.

Injury Prevention

If you've ever had an injury, you know that the forced period of inactivity is frustrating. Putting your workouts on hold while your injured body part heals can be a significant setback. Your fitness level and conditioning deteriorates, your strength diminishes, and your hard-earned muscle size melts away before your eyes. Not being able to exercise can make you irritable and depressed—workout withdrawal is real. You can avoid all this by taking precautions to reduce your chance of injury. Injury precautions should be a part of everyone's workout routine. Being safe makes perfect sense. Here are some tips to prevent injury:

- ▶ Warm up first with five minutes of stretching or cardio.
- ▶ Avoid massive weights. You must be able to perform at least six reps.
- ▶ Increase weight gradually, no more than 5 percent at a time.
- ▶ Keep workouts under an hour.
- ▶ Take one rest day each week.
- ▶ Cycle the intensity of your workouts (periodization).
- ▶ Train at a well-equipped gym.
- ▶ Use machines for greatest safety.
- ▶ Maintain correct technical form.
- ▶ Stop for sharp pain. Recognize the first signs of injury.

A little gentle stretching will help warm up the body and prevent injury.

The risk of injury is greater at certain times. I call them windows for disaster. Such times are like driving on the freeway in heavy rain. Ease off the gas pedal. Exercise extreme caution when

▶ you're sick or more tired than usual,

▶ you train at a different time of day,

▶ you train during cold weather,

▶ you train at a new or unfamiliar gym, or

▶ you try a new exercise or a different piece of equipment.

Such times are probably not the greatest for trying for a new personal best. If you feel really tired or sick, substitute a scheduled weight workout with some gentle cardio or take an extra rest day. During cold weather, remember that your body needs a longer warm-up period and a few extra clothes to maintain body heat. Whenever you try a new exercise or equipment, there's a learning curve involved, so use lighter weights until you know what you're doing.

Injury First Aid

What should you do if you get injured? The first aid treatment for any injury aims to relieve pain, inflammation, and swelling. Follow six simple steps, which you can remember by the acronym PRICED (protect, rest, ice, compression, elevation, drugs):

▶ **Protect.** Stop the offending exercise immediately to prevent further damage from occurring.

▶ **Rest.** Restrict the use of the injured limb. When the injury involves your hip, knee, or ankle, walk only if absolutely necessary and use a cane or crutches to minimize the weight placed on the leg.

▶ **Ice.** Apply an ice pack to the painful area for 10 to 15 minutes, repeating three or four times each day during the first 48 hours after injury.

▶ **Compression.** An elastic support keeps swelling to a minimum. Compression should not be too tight and must be removed intermittently to allow blood circulation. There's no need to wear the support when sleeping at night.

▶ **Elevation.** Elevating the limb uses gravity to improve blood flow back to the heart, aiding drainage of the fluid that causes swelling. The higher the elevation, the better the fluid drainage.

▶ **Drugs.** An anti-inflammatory medication, such as ibuprofen, helps relieve pain. Always read the label first and follow the instructions. I usually recommend 400 milligrams of ibuprofen three times a day for a week following injury. Many anti-inflammatories are not recommended for people with stomach ulcers, asthma, or bleeding disorders.

You need to recognize the first signs of injury. Learn to distinguish the sharp pain arising from a joint or tendon from the burning ache of muscle fatigue. Any sharp pain is a warning sign saying back off or slow down. The safest response is to stop for sharp pain. Quit that exercise or even your whole workout. Follow the PRICED treatment procedure. Go home, apply some ice to the painful area, and take an anti-inflammatory medication. If the pain persists, see your doctor. Don't risk making the injury worse. Be attentive. Listen to the signals your body is sending. Treat any pain with respect.

If the pain, swelling, or bruising is severe, it's better to seek medical attention sooner rather than later. If you want an accurate diagnosis and the best treatment, there's no substitute for a proper medical evaluation. This involves a careful physical exam and an X-ray of the injured area to rule out a bone fracture. Further tests such as an ultrasound or MRI scan can help evaluate damage to the soft tissues of muscle, tendon, and ligament. The correct diagnosis is necessary for choosing the most effective treatment.

MUSCLE MAINTENANCE

It's easier to maintain the changes you make to your body than it is to create them in the first place. Bodybuilding is like hiking on a mountain. With each difficult step upward you make progress, but once you've got your footing, it doesn't take much effort to hold your ground.

There are many paths up the mountain. Depending on your goals, you can head in the direction of muscle mass or switch your destination toward fat loss. Providing you stay on the well-trodden paths, you'll avoid sliding back down the slippery slope. Still, you're bound to encounter a few unforeseen obstacles along the route. There will be demons—overtraining, injury, lack of discipline, loss of motivation—perched on your shoulder, tempting you toward disaster. What you need to ward off these demons is a maintenance plan, a strategy to thwart disaster and guide you around the obstacles. Maintaining your body is easy if you know how.

A perfect physique requires several key ingredients mixed in the right measures, brewed in the best environment, and nurtured over time. None of these steps can be left to chance. If you neglect even the smallest detail, you won't turn out a classic sculpture. Use the following 10-point problem-solution checklist to prevent pitfalls and remedy the problems that impede your bodybuilding progress.

Incorporate Variety

The problem: muscle boredom. The solution: muscle confusion.

We've all heard that variety is the spice of life. Well, this pearl of wisdom applies to your muscles, too. You see, muscles are incredibly adaptive to exercise, and they respond to one type of training for only a limited time. Persisting with the same routine indefinitely condemns you to physique stagnation. Your muscles get bored. Sticking to the same exercises out of habit or an unwillingness to change keeps you fixed at the same level of development.

A solution to muscle boredom is muscle confusion. To break free of a training plateau, shock your muscles by asking them to do something they haven't done before. Changing your exercise stimulus forces your muscles to adapt to new demands.

Incorporating variety into your exercise program keeps your workout fresh. Change your exercises or the structure of your workout. Confuse your muscles by giving them a challenge they haven't faced before. Avoid the same old routine; keep your muscles guessing.

With each workout, make small changes to the exercise content and order. For example, you can do bench presses using a standard barbell, a pair of dumbbells, or a machine. You can do biceps curls using a straight bar, dumbbells, cables, or a machine. Changing the way you do an exercise from one workout to the next forces your muscles to adapt on a regular basis. Your muscles don't become stale—and you won't get bored—from doing the same old exercises.

Keep a pool of your favorite exercises for each muscle group and select a different movement each time you work out. The best workouts are the ones that keep challenging your muscles.

Sculpt Proportionally

The problem: a lagging body part. The solution: priority training.

An eye-catching physique requires more than just mass. Individual muscle groups must be developed in proportion. Sure, every bodybuilder wants big biceps—those huge arms are always on display in the "shop window." But if your bulging biceps overshadow your chest and shoulder development, you're not displaying a crafted physique. Heads may turn at the sight of bulging muscles, but jaws drop in the presence of sculpted body work.

A balanced, proportioned physique looks amazing, but it makes biomechanical sense, too. Muscle imbalances are a fast track to injury. A neglected rotator cuff is a prime example. Ignore these muscles, and a pair of painful shoulders will soon be yours. Instead of blasting away with set after intense set of arm builders, train all your body parts with equal attention.

Despite your diligence to train each muscle group with equal intensity, you might discover that some body parts respond better to exercise than others. Even professional bodybuilders suffer the plague of lagging body parts. Sometimes the culprit is subconscious neglect, but more often the problem is genetic. Certain muscle groups are just wired differently. Some people are blessed with big arms; others are born with king-sized calves. It's worth being objective and recognizing the chink in your armor—you can fix the lagging muscle group through priority training.

Prioritizing the weak area of your physique means paying the area special attention and focus. There are three ways to do this. First, train the underdeveloped body part at the beginning of your workout when your energy level is highest. Second, relocate the weak muscle group to the beginning of a workout week when your body is fresh from the rest period over the weekend. Third, simply work the lagging muscle more than you work the others.

Cycle Your Workouts

The problem: overtraining. The solution: periodization.

To benefit from regular exercise, you need to do 30 minutes of physical activity at least three times a week. That's bare minimum. On the flip side, if you're exercising for more than an hour each day, seven days a week, you're doing too much. It's virtually impossible for your body to recover fully from each workout on this kind of a schedule, so you won't gain muscle size or strength. Doing too much exercise is counterproductive; it leads to a state of overtraining. When this happens, you stop making progress, get weaker, and leave yourself wide open to injury. Remember that your muscles must recover from the exercise stimulus in order to reap the benefits. More is not necessarily better. And don't make your regime more complicated than it needs to be. Keep it simple. If you think you're overtraining, take this little quiz to be sure.

ARE YOU OVERTRAINING?

1. Do you always feel tired?   YES   NO
2. Are you losing muscle size?   YES   NO
3. Have you lost strength?   YES   NO
4. Are your muscles tender?   YES   NO
5. Has your appetite decreased?   YES   NO
6. Do you have difficulty sleeping?   YES   NO
7. Do your workouts lack energy?   YES   NO
8. Do you lack motivation?   YES   NO

If you answered yes to more than three questions, you might be overtraining. If you answered yes to more than five questions, you're very likely overtraining.

The solution to overtraining is periodization. Periodization is the process of cycling the intensity and format of your workouts. This technique gives you flexibility to make adjustments in your training regime. You can make cyclic changes over short monthly intervals or on a longer seasonal basis.

In the short term, you should cycle your workout intensity. After four to six weeks of high-intensity training, ease off the gas pedal and reduce intensity for a couple of weeks. This periodic down time provides two major benefits. First, your body gets a rest, which helps prevent overtraining and injury. Second, your mind gets a rest, which helps maintain motivation. Intense workouts are extremely demanding; down time helps prevent burnout.

In the long term, you can change the focus of your training program on a seasonal basis. For instance, you might choose to bulk up during the winter season using the mass generator program (chapter 4). In the spring, you could switch to the body fat blitz program (chapter 7). During the summer, you can flip over to the hybrid hard body program (chapter 11) to look your best on the beach. Then during the fall, select a period of low intensity to give your body some respite.

It doesn't matter how you cycle the intensity of your workouts or when you switch from one program to another. The important thing is that you do incorporate periodization in your game plan. Changing the intensity and focus of your workouts on a regular basis is a key factor for continued progress as well as preventing overtraining.

Stay Nutritionally Sound

The problem: using the wrong fuel. The solution: dietary discipline.

Anything you put in your mouth should serve a nutritional purpose, not just satisfy your hunger or appeal to your taste buds. Don't waste your calorie count on useless junk. For instance, a doughnut has no real nutritional benefit. Sure, it tastes good and provides a small sugar rush, but that glazed ring of candy becomes a spare tire around your waist. It has no muscle-building benefit at all. You wouldn't pour sugar into your car's gas tank, would you? If you're going to eat something, make it worthwhile. Junk food is body pollution. You don't litter anywhere else, so why litter your body?

To prevent nutritional setbacks, use dietary discipline. If you're not gaining muscle or losing fat, the first thing to do is review your calorie intake and check your daily calorie requirement. Then check the content of your diet and the ratio of protein, carbohydrates, and fat. Make sure you comply with the recommendations in your diet plan.

There's no quick fix diet or magic pill for fat loss and muscle gain. If you want healthy, lasting results, you need to change your lifestyle. Follow these tips to keep your diet on track:

▶ **Keep a cookbook.** Writing down your personal diet plan is essential for success. Calculate your daily calorie requirement (body weight in pounds × 10) and consume six small meals at three- to four-hour intervals during the day. Write down your meal schedule, record the content of each meal, and stick to the plan. To facilitate fat loss, the ratio of macronutrients in your diet should be about 50 percent protein, 40 percent carbohydrates, and 10 percent fat. Consume at least one gram of protein per pound of body weight each day.

▶ **Eat clean to be lean.** Clean food is devoid of any unnecessary additives and thus has no hidden calories. For example, a plain grilled chicken breast is clean, whereas a piece of fried chicken in breadcrumbs is not. Similarly, a baked potato is clean, but a plate of fries is loaded with fat calories. Keeping your diet simple makes it easier to monitor calories. Processed foods such as mayonnaise contain lots of salt, fat, and preservatives. Sauces and flavorings should be low fat and used sparingly.

▶ **Keep it simple.** The focus of your attention should be on the protein, carbohydrates, fat, and calorie content of food. Don't get bogged down by small, unnecessary details. It wastes your time and distracts you from the big picture.

▶ **Shop to succeed.** Don't go to the grocery store hungry. Make a list and stick to it. If it's not on your list of authorized foods, don't even pick it up. When your house is free of junk food, you'll be less likely to have a damaging snack attack. Keep junk food out of sight, out of mind.

▶ **Read the label.** Calculating food portions and calories is easy if you read the product label. Pay close attention to what constitutes a serving because the calorie content is based on this amount. If a product doesn't have a label with nutrition facts, don't eat it unless it came from a tree or the ground.

▶ **Pack a snack.** Eating small meals every three to four hours means you'll sometimes eat outside your home. Go prepared! Pack several small meals or snacks to take to work. Meal-replacement drinks, protein shakes or bars, and fruit are useful for this purpose. Pack enough supplies to avoid hunger pangs and the temptation of junk food.

▶ **Consume everything in moderation.** No matter what you eat, never gorge yourself until your belly pops your buttons off. One helping is enough. Stuffing yourself bloats your belly and protrudes your waistline. Excess calories consumed at one sitting get stored as fat.

▶ **Think before you drink.** Your average eight-ounce beverage contains at least 100 calories, whether it's soda, fruit juice, milk, or beer. During the course of the day, it's easy to drink away almost half of your daily calorie intake. The solution to this pollution is water. Remember that 70 percent of your muscle is water, and you should drink at least a gallon of water every day to maintain hydration. The caffeine in coffee and tea can aid fat loss, and these beverages are low in calories if you don't add milk or sugar. If you crave soda, make sure your choice is low in calories.

▶ **Be prepared when dining out.** Eating healthfully at a restaurant is not impossible. Substitute unhealthful side dishes such as fries with a small salad or steamed rice. Ask for sauces and dressings to be placed on the side. Dip your fork into the dressing and then take a bite of your food. It's a great way to keep the flavor without getting the excess calories. If there are no substitutions, try to build a meal from the healthier single side orders on the menu. When all else fails, find another place to eat. Remember that you do have one cheat day per week. If you want to make dining out a feast to remember, use your cheat day to order whatever you want.

▶ **Use supplements intelligently.** Eating a nutritious diet is far more important than the supplements you take. Supplements add to your diet; they don't take the place of it. There are useful supplements that can help. For instance, meal-replacement drinks are convenient when you're on the go. Protein shakes top off your protein intake, and liquid is easily digested when you replenish after a workout. A bite or two from a low-carb protein bar is an acceptable way to curb cravings between meals. A multivitamin or mineral supplement helps prevent dietary deficiencies. Adequate consumption of vitamins B, C, and E aids exercise and recovery.

▶ **Set short-term goals.** Rather than thinking of your nutrition plan as a diet, think of it as changing the way you eat. Take your time and be patient. Start by setting daily goals. Eliminate desserts, candy, and other unhealthful snacks. Replace soda with water. Select low-fat alternatives. Then tackle the goals that might take longer to accomplish. Gradually cut back on carbohydrates and increase protein in your diet. Monitor your progress with a weekly weight check on the bathroom scale and a monthly body fat measurement with a skin caliper. Take small steps in the right direction.

▶ **Don't get caught in a fad.** Forget about secrets or shortcuts in dieting. There aren't any. Most fad diets work only in the short term. If you want to lose weight and keep it off, you have to make lasting lifestyle changes. Learn to cook, shop, and dine in a healthful way, and those pounds will stay off.

▶ **Forgive your mistakes.** We all have our vices. If you fall off the wagon and engage in a weekend of beer and pizza, don't panic. If you make a mistake, you can't really compensate by overexercising or starving yourself. Let mistakes be bygones, get back on schedule, and keep moving forward. Don't let setbacks or mistakes slow you down, but do try to learn from your indiscretions.

Get Your Sleep

The problem: lethargy. The solution: rest and recovery.

If you feel constantly tired or lack energy for your workouts, check your sleeping habits. Today's dollar-driven, fast-paced lifestyle leaves many of us in a state of chronic sleep deprivation. People don't sleep enough to recharge their batteries, which results in lethargy and suboptimal levels of performance. Remember that growth and recovery happen while you sleep.

If you're exercising regularly, your body needs seven to eight hours of sleep each night to allow repair mechanisms to do their job. Adequate sleep is especially important if you're trying to build muscle. If you have to rise at the crack of dawn to get to work, make sure you go to bed early the night before. Resist the temptation to stay up late socializing or watching TV. Make getting enough sleep a high priority. If you can't fit in eight hours of sleep overnight, seize any opportunity during the day to take a 30- to 60-minute power nap to recharge your batteries. You'll feel more refreshed for the rest of the day. Whatever happens, don't let chronic sleep deprivation hamper your progress.

Increase Intensity

The problem: lacking mass. The solution: intensify.

If you're not packing on pounds of muscle, you're not putting enough effort into your training. When at the gym, do you train your butt off or just go through the motions? To make progress, you have to keep challenging yourself, continually pushing your body to new limits.

Muscle growth requires a hypertrophic stimulus. That means six to eight reps performed to failure. To continually challenge your muscles, train beyond failure with the techniques that generate added intensity (see chapter 8). Without intensity, muscles won't grow.

Keep Your Focus

The problem: you're easily distracted. The solution: stay focused.

Add intensity to pack on muscle mass.

If you want to benefit from your workouts, you simply can't waste time at the gym. To achieve the best results, keep your workouts short, sweet, and intense. When you're not lifting a weight, you're catching your breath and lining up the next exercise. There's no time for gossip or reading a book. If you waste more than two minutes between sets or exercises, you won't get your workout done on time. Before you know it, you're spending over an hour in the gym. No way can you fulfill your best workouts if you're constantly catching up on gossip. Oversocializing wastes precious gym time and extends your workouts needlessly.

If you're easily distracted, take steps to prevent it. Avoid making eye contact. Wear stereo headphones while you train to discourage interruptions. Get serious. Switch off your cell phone; there's nothing that can't wait 30 minutes while you complete your workout. An effective workout demands your full attention, so don't corrupt it.

Stay Clean

The problem: contamination. The solution: just say no.

It goes without saying that alcohol and substance abuse affects your health and fitness. We're talking about recreational drugs here, not those prescribed for medical reasons by your doctor. Alcohol affects exercise performance and recovery. It's also a source of useless and unnecessary calories. It doesn't matter how meticulous you are with food intake; if you're drinking a few servings of alcohol every day, you won't reduce body fat. A few bottles of beer or some wine over the weekend won't hurt, but be moderate.

Cigarette smoking impairs lung function and reduces the oxygen supply to your muscles. You can't perform to the best of your abilities if you're polluting your lungs on a daily basis. Similarly, recreational drugs such as marijuana adversely affect exercise performance and your body's ability to recover. You can't become a high-performance machine if you're voluntarily contaminating your body.

For a whole host of health reasons, abstinence is best. If you want to make the best possible progress with your fitness goals, just say no to drugs and alcohol.

Take a Short Break

The problem: a lack of time. The solution: down time.

Your training commitment amounts to less than five hours per week. Even the busiest of work schedules can accommodate a daily 30-minute workout. However, there will be circumstances that interfere with gym time, including vacations, ill health, domestic difficulties, work deadlines, and business trips. With careful planning, your muscle-building progress should not suffer.

Everyone needs down time once in a while, and a short break from your workout schedule won't interfere with your progress. However, apply two rules when taking timeouts. First, they should last no longer than a week or two. Second, don't take them too frequently. Exercise and diet must be maintained on a regular basis. Your workout program is only as effective as your last bout of exercise, and your diet is only as healthy as your last meal. Muscles adapt to the demands placed on them. If you stop exercising, muscle shrinks and loses its strength.

A short interruption won't have adverse effects on your overall progress. If you stop exercising for a week, you won't lose significant muscle size or strength. In fact, a seven-day period of complete rest allows your body to restock muscle fuel and heal nagging injuries. Aches and pains disappear or diminish, and when you resume exercising, you'll feel stronger and more energetic. But there's a fine line between a short therapeutic rest and an extended layoff. Two weeks is probably the longest time you can safely take off without compromising strength and fitness. If you take a longer timeout, you'll lose conditioning, which makes it tough to get back on course when you resume your workouts.

If you stop exercising for longer than two weeks, your muscles atrophy and decrease in size and strength. Muscles don't turn to fat—this is physically impossible because muscle and fat are two completely different tissues. What happens when you stop exercising is that you continue eating the same amount of food, but you don't burn as many calories. The excess calories get stored as fat. If you want to avoid gaining

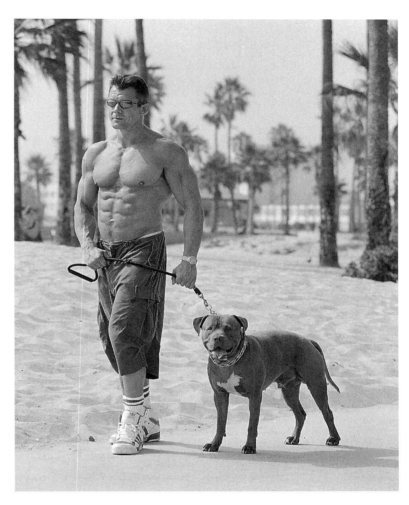

Plan some down time, but keep it short.

weight when you stop exercising, reduce the amount of calories you consume to match your reduced calorie expenditure.

The bottom line is that a short timeout is acceptable when taken infrequently. You can allow yourself a week off every three to four months or a total of four weeks a year. If you let your exercise program or diet lapse for longer periods, you'll lose your conditioning. So, when you must call a timeout, use it wisely.

Another solution to a lack of time is a busybody workout. During times when family or work commitments become demanding, downsize your workout schedule to accommodate them. Staying in shape doesn't require as much time as most people think. Four 30-minute workouts each week is all you need to maintain an exercise commitment.

When your time is required elsewhere, you can make do with two simple 30-minute in-and-out workout routines. The first workout is indoor weight-training aimed at working your upper body. Choose one exercise to work each of the six major muscle groups of your torso and arms (chest, shoulders, back, biceps, triceps, abs). For example, you might do bench presses, dumbbell side laterals, lat pulldowns (or chin-ups), biceps curls, triceps pushdowns, and sit-ups. Your second workout of the week involves an indoor or outdoor cardio exercise of your choice to burn fat and shape your legs. Choose from exercises such as cycling, walking, jogging, or stair climbing.

TRAVEL TIPS

To prevent those business trips (or vacations) from disrupting your workout program and diet, my top travel tip is go prepared! Maintaining dietary discipline during travel is not difficult if you use some convenient nutrition supplements. Before leaving home, pack a 24- to 48-hour supply of quality supplements. For the plane ride, pack a couple of ready-to-drink protein shakes and a handful of protein bars. Your carry-on bag should also contain a bottle of water because you'll dehydrate quickly on the plane, which can aggravate jet lag. Pack as many sachets of meal-replacement powder as you can carry in your checked luggage. These are lifesavers when you arrive at your destination because the powder mixes easily with water in your hotel room.

If you're away for more than a couple of days, check the phone book for the nearest health food store so you can restock on supplements. This way you don't have to overload your luggage. During your hotel stay, try to find a grocery store for some easy-to-eat items such as cans or packets of water-packed tuna and a carton of nonfat milk. In most cities, you can hunt down at least one or two restaurants that cater to the health conscious.

As for exercise, most good hotels have an exercise room. Bring your lightweight workout gear. Even with the busiest of schedules, you should be able to fit in 30 minutes on the stationary bicycle. If the hotel health spa isn't to your liking, check the phone book to see if there's a good gym in town. If you're in a motel in the middle of nowhere, you'll have to make do with a brisk 30-minute walk or swim and maybe some pushups and sit-ups. A little exercise is better than none at all.

The bottom line when traveling is that you can maintain an element of discipline in your diet and exercise routine with some thoughtful planning.

Pump Up Motivation

The problem: a poor attitude. The solution: get motivated.

If you don't believe you can make progress, chances are you won't. You need a strong conviction in your ability. Believe that you're capable of more, and you'll achieve it. Lacking conviction will slowly infect all aspects of your exercise and nutrition program. It influences your intensity, dampens your discipline, and lets you neglect nutrition. Lack of motivation has a domino effect, knocking down all aspects of your progress.

Do everything in your power to control your attitude. Eliminate doubts or negative thoughts that might be holding you back, preventing you from reaching your full potential. The ABCs of self-motivation are action, belief, and consistency.

▶ **Action.** Now that you've read this book, you have the knowledge you need to develop the ultimate body. Knowledge is indeed the key, but you have to put the key in the lock, open the door, and make it happen. It's easy to talk the talk, but you also must walk the walk. Turn your thoughts into action. Actions speak louder than words, and you must act to get the job done. Why dawdle? You have been wanting this for years. Do it.

▶ **Belief.** Believe to achieve. Everyone has potential—you've just got to make it happen. Snooze and lose. Strive and come alive. Use the bumper sticker that works for you. Believe in yourself and your capabilities. Nearly anything is possible if you want it bad enough.

▶ **Consistency.** Nothing happens overnight. It takes great willpower to stick with an exercise program and change your dietary habits, but you've got to stick with it. You have to be consistent, persistent, and patient. Great things come to those who wait. The change will happen; just give it a chance. To help yourself be consistent, make your workout schedule convenient. Select a time of day that works best for you; choose a gym that's conveniently located. The further you have to travel to the gym, the less likely you'll make the journey. Don't give yourself any excuses.

▶ **Discipline.** We're all creatures of habit. No matter how flexible you are, I bet there's some element of routine in your day-to-day living, a basic structure around which everything else revolves. We eat, drink, and sleep every day. Most of us have to work to earn a living, and we fit in some play time when possible. Without structure, there's chaos. Without rules, there's disorder. To build a better body, all you must do is make slight adjustments to your daily routine. Just add that little extra bit of discipline. Squeeze in a 30-minute workout; sprinkle some healthy spice into your diet. Come on, it's easy! If I can do it, anyone can. Take small steps at first. Just keep saying to yourself, "I can do this. I will do this. I have the discipline it takes."

▶ **Evolution.** Your body evolves, and you have to change with it. You'll become stronger, fitter, and ready to rise to the next level to meet new challenges. It's all about progress. If you're not making progress, step back and take a critical look at what's holding you back. Isolate the problem and fix it. Don't get stuck in a rut. Keep moving up the ladder. Strive to climb further up the hill; the view just gets better and better.

▶ **Faults.** We all have our faults. No one is perfect. Whatever happens, don't let faults or mistakes hold you back. If you were not blessed with meaty arms, and they won't grow as fast as you'd like, don't throw in the towel. Rethink your arm workout; change your exercises. Maybe you're not using the right bait. Try to keep your exercise program and diet as simple as possible. Don't make something more complicated than it has to be. Some people suffer from information overload. They accumulate so much that they end up getting confused and can't see the wood through the trees. Simple exercise and diet regimes are often more effective than complicated ones. If you do make a mistake—miss a workout or binge on pizza—don't fret. What's done is done. Acknowledge your mistake and learn from it—then cast it aside and get back to your program.

▶ **Goals.** Nothing is more motivating than witnessing progress. Scoring a goal is a great feeling, a reward for your efforts. But to reach a goal, you must set it in the first place. Without goals, you have no direction. To make your goal real, be diligent with documentation. When you keep a weekly record of measurements, such as strength, body weight, and body fat percentage, you can accurately chart your progress. Quick, objective measurements like these are better than subjective impressions, such as looking in the mirror, where visible changes tend to occur more slowly. If you want a regular income of motivation, set and record your short-term goals. Be realistic, take small steps at first, and enjoy monitoring your progress.

Finally, one last word. Enjoy. To do something regularly, you need to enjoy it. If you enjoy your exercise program, you won't need further motivation. Do everything in your power to make your workout experience enjoyable. Join a gym with a good atmosphere, train with a motivated workout buddy, or play your favorite music on a personal stereo. Choose exercises that you actually like doing; if you enjoy the exercise, it will work for you. Enjoy your gym time. Sculpt your body. Stay healthy. Be happy. Start now. That's a doctor's order.

FOOD NUTRITION FACTS

Values are approximate. Check the nutrition facts label on individual brands. These foods are featured in the sample meal plans in chapters 4, 7, and 11. Proteins are listed first, followed by starchy carbohydrates and fibrous carbohydrates.

Food	Protein	Carbohydrates	Fat	Calories
Chicken breast (6 oz)	35	0	6	200
Lean beef (6 oz)	35	0	6	200
Turkey breast (6 oz)	35	0	3	180
Tuna, water-packed (6 oz)	35	0	2	160
Egg white (1)	6	0	0	24
Nonfat milk (240 ml)	9	12	0	90
Rice (50 g)	3	39	0	170
Pasta (50 g)	6	40	1	200
Potato (1 medium)	2	35	0	160
Oats (40 g)	5	27	3	150
Carrots (80 g)	1	9	0	40
Broccoli (80 g)	1	4	0	20
Spinach (80 g)	2	3	0	20
Whole-wheat bread (1 slice)	4	18	2	110
Low-fat granola	4	36	4	200

TRAINING, NUTRITION, AND PROGRESS CHARTS

Make copies of the following charts to plan and record your workouts, diet, and progress.

Training Log

Date	Muscle	Exercise	Set 1 (weight × reps)	Set 2 (weight × reps)	Set 3 (weight × reps)

Notes:

Workout time:

Personal Diet Chart

Meal	Time	Food	Calories	Protein	Carbohydrates	Fat
1						
2						
3						
4						
5						
6						
		Totals (per day)				

Progress Chart

Measurement	Time						
	Start	1 month	2 months	3 months	4 months	5 months	6 months
Body weight							
Body fat %							

Size
    Waist
    Chest
    Arms
    Thighs							

Cardio time							
Strength (6 reps) Bench press Squat Biceps curl							

Notes:

bibliography

EXERCISE AND MUSCLE HYPERTROPHY

Campos, G.E., Luecke, T.J., Wendeln, H.K., Toma, K., Hagerman, F.C., Murray, T.F., Ragg, K.E., Ratamess, N.A., Kraemer, W.J., and Staron, R.S. 2002. Muscular adaptations in response to three different resistance-training regimens: Specificity of repetition maximum training zones. *Eur J Appl Physiol* 88:50-60.

Chestnut, J.L., and Docherty, D. 1999. The effect of 4 and 10 repetition maximum weight-training protocols on neuromuscular adaptations in untrained men. *J Strength Cond Res* 13:353-359.

Gibala, M.J., Interisano, S.A., Tarnopolsky, M.A., Roy, B.D., MacDonald, J.R., Yarasheski, K.E., and MacDougall, J.D. 2000. Myofibrillar disruption following acute concentric and eccentric resistance exercise in strength-trained men. *Can J Physiol Pharmacol* 78:656-661.

Hass C.J., Garzarella, L., de Hoyos, D., and Pollock, M.L. 2000. Single versus multiple sets in long-term recreational weightlifters. *Med Sci Sports Exerc* 32:235-242.

Kraemer, W.J., Marchitelli, L., Gordon, S.E., Harman, E., Dziados, J.E., Mello, R., Frykman, P., McCurry, D., and Fleck, S.J. 1990. Hormonal and growth factor response to heavy resistance exercise protocols. *J Appl Physiol* 69:1442-1450.

Kramer, J.B., Stone, M.H., O'Bryant, H.S., Conley, M.S., Johnson, R.L., Nieman, D.C., Honeycutt, D.R., and Hoke T.P. 1997. Effects of single vs. multiple sets of weight training: Impact of volume, intensity, and variation. *J Strength Cond Res* 11:143-147.

MacDougall, J.D., Gibala, M.J., Tarnopolsky, M.A., MacDonald, J.R., Interisano, S.A., and Yarasheski, K.E. 1995. The time course for elevated muscle protein synthesis following heavy resistance exercise. *Can J Appl Physiol* 20:480-486.

McCall, G.E., Byrnes, W.C., Dickinson, A., Pattany, P.M., and Fleck, S.J. 1996. Muscle fiber hypertrophy, hyperplasia, and capillary density in college men after resistance training. *J Appl Physiol* 81:2004-2012.

Rhea, M.R., Alvar, B.A., Ball, S.D., and Burkett, L.N. 2002. Three sets of weight training superior to 1 set with equal intensity for eliciting strength. *J Strength Cond Res* 16:525-529.

Westcott, W.L., Winett, R.A., Anderson, E.S., Wojcik, J.R., Loud, R.L., Cleggett, E., and Glover, S. 2001. Effects of regular and slow speed resistance training on muscle strength. *J Sports Med Phys Fitness* 41:154-158.

Williams, A.G., Ismail, A.N., Sharma, A., and Jones, D.A. 2002. Effects of resistance exercise volume and nutritional supplementation on anabolic and catabolic hormones. *Eur J Appl Physiol* 86:315-321.

ANABOLIC STEROIDS

Bhasin, S., Storer, T.W., Berman, N., Callegari, C., Clevenger, B., Phillips, J., Bunnell, T.J., Tricker, R., Shirazi, A., and Casaburi, R. 1996. The effects of supraphysiological doses of testosterone on muscle size and strength in normal men. *N Eng J Med* 335:1-7.

Bhasin, S., Woodhouse, L., Casaburi, R., Singh, A.B., Bhasin, D., Berman, N., Chen, X., Yarasheski, K.E., Magliano, L., Dzekov, C., Dzekov, J., Bross, R., Phillips, J., Sinha-Hikim, I., Shen, R., and Storer, T.W. 2001. Testosterone dose-response relationships in healthy young men. *Am J Physiol Endocrinol Metab* 281:E1172-E1181.

Evans, N.A. 1997. Gym and tonic: A profile of 100 male steroid users. *Br J Sports Med* 31:54-58.

Evans, N.A. 1997. Local complications of self-administered anabolic steroid injections. *Br J Sports Med* 31:349-350.

Evans, N.A. In press. Current concepts in anabolic-androgenic steroids. *Am J Sports Med* 31.

Evans, N.A., Bowrey, D.J., and Newman, G.R. 1998. Ultrastructural analysis of ruptured tendon from anabolic steroid users. *Injury* 29:769-773.

Sinha-Hikim, I., Artaza, J., Woodhouse, L., Gonzalez-Cadavid, N., Singh, A.B., Lee, M.I., Storer, T.W., Casaburi, R., Shen, R., and Bhasin, S. 2002. Testosterone-induced increase in muscle size in healthy young men is associated with muscle fiber hypertrophy. *Am J Physiol Endocrinol Metab* 283:E154-E164.

Sturmi, J.E., and Diorio, D.J. 1998. Anabolic Agents. *Clin Sports Med* 17:261-282.

NUTRITION AND SUPPLEMENTS

Boozer, C.N., Daly, P.A., Homel, P., Solomon, J.L., Blanchard, D., Nasser, J.A., Strauss, R., and Meredith, T. 2002. Herbal ephedra/caffeine for weight loss: A 6-month randomized safety and efficacy trial. *Int J Obes Relat Metab Disord* 26:593-604.

Brief, A.A., Maurer, S.G., and Di Cesare, P.E. 2001. Use of glucosamine and chondroitin sulphate in the management of osteoarthritis. *J Am Acad Orthop Surg* 9:71-78.

Burke, D.G., Chilibeck, P.D., Davidson, K.S., Candow, D.G., Farthing, J., and Smith-Palmer, T. 2001. The effect of whey protein supplementation with and without creatine monohydrate combined with resistance training on lean tissue mass and muscle strength. *Int J Sport Nutr Exerc Metab* 11:349-364.

Broeder, C.E. 2003. Oral andro-related prohormone supplementation: Do the potential risks outweigh the benefits? *Can J Appl Physiol* 28:102-116.

Catlin, D.H., Leder, B.Z., Ahrens, B., Starcevic, B., Hatton, C.K., Green, G.A., and Finkelstein, J.S. 2000. Trace contamination of over-the-counter androstenedione and positive urine test results for a nandrolone metabolite. *JAMA* 284:2618-2621.

Delbeke, F.T., Van Eenoo, P., Van Thuyne, W., and Desmet, N. 2003. Prohormones and sport. *J Steroid Biochem Mol Biol* 83:245-251.

King, D.S., Sharp, R.L., Vukovich, M.D., Brown, G.A., Reifenrath, T.A., Uhl, N.L., and Parsons, K.A. 1999. Effect of oral androstenedione on serum testosterone and adaptations to resistance training in young men. *JAMA* 281:2020-2028.

Kreider, R.B., Melton, C., Rasmussen, C.J., Greenwood, M., Lancaster, S., Cantler, E.C., Milnor, P., and Almada, A.L. 2003. Long-term creatine supplementation does not significantly affect clinical markers of health in athletes. *Mol Cell Biochem* 244:95-104.

Lawrence, M.E., and Kirby, D.F. 2002. Nutrition and sports supplements: Fact or fiction. *J Clin Gastroenterol* 35:299-306.

Leder, B.Z., Longcope, C., Catlin, D.H., Ahrens, B., Schoenfeld, D.A., and Finkelstein, J.S. 2000. Oral androstenedione administration and serum testosterone concentrations in young men. *JAMA 283*:779-782.

Nissen, S.L., and Sharp, R.L. 2003. Effect of dietary supplements on lean mass and strength gains with resistance exercise: A meta-analysis. *J Appl Physiol* 94:651-659.

Reginster, J.Y., Deroisy, R., Rovati, L.C., Lee, R.L., Lejeune, E., Bruyere, O., Giacovelli, G., Henrotin, Y., Dacre, J.E., and Gossett, C. 2001. Long-term effects of glucosamine sulphate on osteoarthritis progression: A randomized placebo-controlled trial. *Lancet* 357:251-256.

Roy, B.D., Fowles, J.R., Hill, R., and Tarnopolsky, M.A. 2000. Macronutrient intake and whole body protein metabolism following resistance exercise. *Med Sci Sports Exerc* 32:1412-1418.

Rozenek, R., Ward, P., Long, S., and Garhammer, J. 2002. Effects of high-calorie supplementation on body composition and muscular strength following resistance training. *J Sports Med Phys Fitness* 42:340-347.

Schedel, J.M., Tanaka, H., Kiyonaga, A., Shindo, M., and Schutz, Y. 2000. Acute creatine loading enhances human growth hormone secretion. *J Sports Med Phys Fitness* 40:336-342.

Shekelle, P.G., Hardy, M.L., Morton, S.C., Maglione, M., Mojica, W.A., Suttorp, M.J., Rhodes, S.L., Jungvig, L., and Gagne, J. 2003. Efficacy and safety of ephedra and ephedrine for weight loss and athletic performance. *JAMA* 289:1537-1545.

Silver, M.D. 2001. Use of ergogenic aids by athletes. *J Am Acad Orthop Surg* 9:61-70.

Tarnopolsky, M.A., Atkinson, S.A., MacDougall, J.D., Chesley, A., Phillips, S., and Schwarcz, H.P. 1992. Evaluation of protein requirements for trained strength athletes. *J Appl Physiol* 73:1986-1995.

Tarnopolsky, M.A., Parise, G., Yardley, N.J., Ballantyne, C.S., Olatinji, S., and Phillips, S.M. 2001. Creatine-dextrose and protein-dextrose induce similar strength gains during training. *Med Sci Sports Exerc* 33:2044-2052.

Terjung, R.L., Clarkson, P., Eichner, E.R., Greenhaff, P.L., Hespel, P.J., Israel, R.G., Kraemer, W.J., Meyer, R.A., Spriet, L.L., Tarnopolsky, M.A., Wagenmakers, A.J., and Williams, M.H. 2000. American College of Sports Medicine roundtable. The physiological and health effects of oral creatine supplementation. *Med Sci Sports Exerc* 32:706-717.

Vierck, J.L., Icenoggle, D.L., Bucci, L., and Dodson, M.V. 2003. The effects of ergogenic compounds on myogenic satellite cells. *Med Sci Sports Exerc* 35:769-776.

Volek, J.S., Duncan, N.D., Mazzetti, S.A., Staron, R.S., Putukian, M., Gomez, A.L., Pearson, D.R., Fink, W.J., and Kraemer, W.J. 1999. Performance and muscle fiber adaptations to creatine supplementation and heavy resistance training. *Med Sci Sports Exerc* 31:1147-1156.

Wallace, M.B., Lim, J., Cutler, A., and Bucci, L. 1999. Effects of dehydroepiandrosterone vs. androstenedione supplementation in men. *Med Sci Sports Exerc* 31:1788-1792.

Ziegenfuss, T.N., Berardi, J.M., and Lowery, L.M. 2002. Effects of prohormone supplementation in humans: A review. *Can J Appl Physiol* 27:628-646.

index

Note: The italicized t following page numbers refers to tables.

about the author

Dr. Nick Evans, MD, is an orthopedic surgeon and sports medicine physician in Los Angeles and is a highly regarded authority on strength training, nutrition, and weight-training injuries. He has fostered research in sports injury and performance-enhancing aids and has written for many scientific publications.

A bodybuilder and fitness model, Evans is also a regular magazine columnist. He writes a monthly "Ask the Doctor" column for *MuscleMag International* and has also written for *American Health & Fitness* and *IronMan*. In addition, he is a national spokesman for MuscleTech Research and Development, a major sports nutrition company.

Evans resides in Venice, California.